Your Towns and Cities in the (

Grimsby
in the Great War

Your Towns and Cities in the Great War

Grimsby
in the Great War

Stephen Wade

Pen & Sword
MILITARY

First published in Great Britain in 2015 by
PEN & SWORD MILITARY
an imprint of
Pen and Sword Books Ltd
47 Church Street
Barnsley
South Yorkshire S70 2AS

ISBN 978 1 47383 426 2

A CIP record for this book is available from the British Library.

Printed and bound in England
by CPI Group (UK) Ltd, Croydon, CR0 4YY

Typeset in Times New Roman

Pen & Sword Books Ltd incorporates the imprints of
Pen & Sword Archaeology, Atlas, Aviation, Battleground, Discovery,
Family History, History, Maritime, Military, Naval, Politics, Railways,
Select, Social History, Transport, True Crime, and Claymore Press,
Frontline Books, Leo Cooper, Praetorian Press, Remember When,
Seaforth Publishing and Wharncliffe.
For a complete list of Pen and Sword titles please contact
Pen and Sword Books Limited
47 Church Street, Barnsley, South Yorkshire, S70 2AS, England
E-mail: enquiries@pen-and-sword.co.uk
Website: **www.pen-and-sword.co.uk**

Contents

Introduction
6

Chapter One
1914: EAGER FOR A FIGHT
11

Chapter Two
1915: DEEPENING CONFLICT
35

Chapter Three
1916: TOTAL COMMITMENT
59

Chapter Four
1917: SEEING IT THROUGH
77

Chapter Five
1918: THE FINAL BLOWS
89

Chapter Six
1918–1919: THE PROBLEMS OF PEACE
103

Afterword
115

Acknowledgements and Thanks
117

Biography and Sources
118

Index
124

Introduction

On 29 June 1914, Wilfred Scawen Blunt wrote to his friend: 'There has been another assassination, this time of the heir of the Austrian Emperor. I do not quite know how it affects the political situation.' Blunt was not alone in that ignorance. The event was to trigger a massive world war, and the towns on Britain's east coast were to experience some of the results of that event, just as much as the great cities of Europe were to do. In one sense, something far more significant than the 'political situation' was the result – the death of almost 10 million fighting men from all participant armies and more than 956,000 British dead.

There are so many different ways to see and try to understand the Great War and how and why it began, but perhaps there is something in Austrian writer and journalist Stefan Zweig's opinion, as he wrote his memoirs in 1940:

> If today, thinking it over calmly, we wonder why Europe went to war in 1914, there is not one sensible reason to be found, nor even any real occasion for the war. ... I can explain it only, thinking of that excess of power, by seeing it as a tragic consequence of the internal dynamism that had built up during those forty years of peace, and now demanded release.

Whatever the truth or validity of such arguments put forward by people who were alive at the time of the war, the fact is that Europeans, and indeed people of the former British Empire from all over the globe, are left with family memoirs, pictures and oral history relating to that great conflict. There may be a mass of evidence and memorabilia, and stories have been handed down in their millions, but essentially, the strongest material is that of the home and the locality. The Great War might have been a global conflict but it was also a conglomeration of local history stories, every place having its own heroes, its own sacrifices and its own memorials, from the photos in the attic to the lists of those who died chiselled into stone monuments.

During the first twelve days after the announcement that Britain had declared war on Germany, the diarist W.N.P. Barbellion wrote just three entries: 'All Europe is mobilising. ... Will England join in? ... We all await the result of a battle between two millions of men. The tension makes me physically sick.' Normally, he had a lot to write in his diary, but like almost everyone in Britain after that declaration of war on 4

August, he could think of nothing else, and he imagined something on a huge scale – a war that was encroaching on every area of life. It was to be called the Great War, and as I write this, a century has passed since that fateful beginning, yet the memorials and the ceremonies keep that massive conflict in our minds with a mix of horror and pride.

On that 4 August, the *Daily Mail* front-page headline stated the fact boldly: 'GREAT BRITAIN MOBILISES TODAY'. King George V stood on the balcony at Buckingham Palace and waved to a crowd of 10,000 people, and those people remained there all day. From that point on, there was violent and widespread ill feeling expressed against Germany, and in consequence there was a rising tide of anti-German opinion that led to attacks on shops owned by Germans or those that may only have had a German-sounding name.

The professional army at the outbreak of war was organized in terms of an army in India and one at home; the result of military reforms in the late Victorian years. The army at home had a strength of 138,000 men, with another 146,000 in the Reserves. In addition, there was the Territorial Force of about 251,000 men. Britain's supremacy throughout the nineteenth century had been in her navy, and there had been an intensifying rivalry between the British and German navies since the unification of Germany in 1870. But Britain had developed the feared

The Great Central Railway steamers – some of which were taken and held in Germany at the outbreak of war. *Grimsby Central Library.*

Dreadnought class of battleships, and had twenty-nine of those in 1914, along with another forty active older class of battleships, and large numbers of cruisers, small cruisers and destroyers.

Grimsby, as had always been recognized, was in an ideal position with regard to travel to and from Europe, yet it also had what we would now call a global reach. A handbook from 1890 states: 'From Grimsby docks to Hamburg, Rotterdam, and Antwerp, vessels depart every Wednesday and Saturday evening. ... Three large steamships are regularly engaged in trading between this port and the West Indies.' That geographical position, together with that old seafaring tradition and expertise, made Grimsby a place of special importance in 1914.

People in Grimsby were soon to feel that same mix of fear and excitement that Barbellion had reflected in his diary: by the second week of September that year the *Grimsby Telegraph* announced: 'Important notice to athletes and others. A Chums battalion in Grimsby and district.' The word 'chums' evoked in the young men of the town the kind of adventure and camaraderie they had read about since their boyhood in popular boys' stories. In Denis Healey's autobiography, he writes, 'My love for the sentimental patriotism of Buchan and Newbolt was a natural legacy of the First World War, and was fed by the boys' magazines I read – above all the enormous *Chums* annuals.' There had been novels and picture stories about chums at war or at sea, across the great British Empire; now there were to be chums fighting shoulder to shoulder against the German army, across the Channel. Other adverts were even more direct. In one special publication the appeal was very direct, with these words: 'Serve your country by joining the above battalion with your friends. You are wanted!! Enlistment for the war, age nineteen to thirty-five or forty-five in the case of ex-servicemen.' There was even the added inducement of 'A hutted camp is to be built near Grimsby and preliminary training will be carried out there.'

Grimsby, facing Europe, soon felt that it was close to the action. As early as 6 August, HMS *Amphion* was sunk in the North Sea, and by the end of that first month, there had been naval engagements at the Heligoland Bight. Barely had war been announced before this maritime importance was vividly brought home in Grimsby when two German spies were seen and pursued in the town. One press report described what happened after a sentry at the Admiralty wireless station at Waltham saw two men acting suspiciously:

They were apparently trying to cut the pipes supplying the current.
The sentry immediately challenged them, whereupon both men ran

away. The alarm was raised and the guard turned out. After an exciting chase one of the suspects managed to get away, but the other was caught. During the struggle Private Filbert was injured in the leg with a bayonet and was taken to Grimsby Hospital for treatment.

The captured spy was standing before the magistrate the next day.

As those first events of the war grabbed the attention, what was Grimsby like? A map of the town and the Humber published in 1908 shows how small Great Grimsby and Cleethorpes were compared to their expanse today. In the 1911 Census, the population was recorded as being 74,659. It was a boom town in many respects, as so many of the industries there were expanding, and there was a regular flow of emigrants from Europe, most on their way to Liverpool, partly as a result of the Russian pogroms against Jewish settlements and also from the natural desire for poor people in Europe to contemplate a new life in America.

It was going to be a case of 'Greater Grimsby' being together, finding a unity. Immingham, for instance, just a few miles away, was a recently developed dock of great importance. Sam Fay, later knighted, wrote, 'Here on the Humber we have the case of two seaports which are practically sisters … if Grimsby has flourished, the only logical conclusion to come at is that Immingham must flourish too.' The dock had 1,000 acres, and extended 2? miles by 1 mile. The graving dock was 740 feet long and 56 feet wide.

There had been an electric tramway since 1901, and there were a number of theatres and cinemas, so the Edwardians' typical leisure activities were catered for: listening to bands, going for walks and cycle rides, watching the 'silents' at the picture house and drinking in one of the seventy-nine pubs in the town. The town also had two daily newspapers. In the months before war broke out, there had been the usual events such as musical programmes put on by the 1st Lincoln Artillery Volunteers or the Grimsby Railway Servants' Band, and if you had a night at the theatre, there was 'everything for the ladies' at Fred Boyers' shop, and even more at the vast retail premises of Albert Cook on 43–45 Grimsby Road, known as 'The Grimsby Novelty House'.

There were the great fish docks, of course, run by the Great Central Railway; there were sometimes as many as eight daily express trains to London and other cities, distributing the fish, and around the docks there were 587 steam trawlers and a small number of sailing smacks, perhaps about twenty.

Then, of course, there was the Empire. In British schoolrooms one could see the evidence that England was the centre of a vast global empire, all imperial territory was painted pink on the school maps. In 1912 there was the great Empire Fair held at the Pavilion on Wintringham Road, which was staged to raise funds for the building of a new headquarters for the Unionist Party. The event reflected the dominant passion of the Edwardians: to join together and enjoy themselves. The Fair programme announced that 'The Women's League now numbers no fewer than 3,000 members, whilst the Unionist Association and Club are 6,000 strong.'

In 1914, Grimsby was undoubtedly a progressive, busy, confident place to live and work, but as with virtually all large towns and cities in Britain that had played a part in the huge upheaval we know as the first Industrial Revolution, there was an underbelly: there were concerns about pollution and about public health; there had been debate about the apprenticeship system for the fishing industry, and of course there were problems linked to labour relations. On the whole, when war broke out the town was seen, at least from the seat of government, as a valuable asset to have in the great test that was to come.

Chapter One

1914: Eager for a Fight

As *Grimsby's War Work* – the post-war account of its involvement in the Great War – was to point out, the town made a massive contribution to arms and manpower:

> Grimsby provided about 8,000 men for the various military and naval units. These, for the most part, joined the 10th and 11th Lincolns – which battalions were specially raised by Grimsby in reply to Lord Kitchener's appeal – the fifth, 2/5th and 3/5th Lincolns, the 1st North Midland Brigade Royal Field Artillery and the Lincolnshire Yeomanry.

These various units will appear in the following pages, as events unfold. Certainly, in terms of historical writing, the 'Chums' of Kitchener's 'pals regiments' have taken centre stage, but there are many other fighting men, each with their own story.

A war needs military men, and it needs them at home as well as abroad. In 1914, Britain and her empire had recently been improved and reorganized in terms of her armies and her navy. Since the Cardwell reforms of the 1870s had reshuffled the regiments, forming forces at home and away in a rotation system, the professional army was reduced but ostensibly more efficient. But that leaves out the great British institution of the volunteers.

As far back as 1880, Grimsby had had its volunteer soldiers, a group typical of British towns generally, and the last decades of the nineteenth century saw marked increases in the ranks of volunteers in rifle clubs and patriotic groups of all kinds. There had been a gradual development of rivalry with Germany, and a preoccupation with the defence of the British homeland after Germany's massive investment in its navy during that period. In 1890, for instance, a Grimsby publication noted that there were two corps of citizen soldiers in 1887, 'who for manly courage and general efficiency are quite competent to do their part in defending the hearths and homes of their native land in the event of a foreign invasion.'

That tradition of a town having standby volunteers, ready for any military or policing work, was there when war broke out. The Grimsby and Cleethorpes Volunteer Training Corps, while it may not have been

A posed photo intended to make Lord Kitchener's appeal for recruits rather more appealing.
Grimsby Central Library

given the attention in print that the Grimsby Chums have, was an absolutely essential part of the immediate preparations following the outbreak of war with Germany.

It was led by Colonel Harry James Crosby, managing director of Hewitt's Brewery and of the Palace Theatre, and he had two cadres: the older men, too old to serve over the sea, and a cadet group aged from fourteen to eighteen. This force was needed as soon as there was a potential threat from the enemy across the North Sea. The men were drilled and trained at the drill hall in Doughty Road, and of course they were required promptly, as soon as places and possessions needed guarding. The shoreline was a priority, mainly for the gun batteries in place, and when the airship attacks began, the volunteers were the men to work with the guns and the searchlights.

The parallels with the Second World War Home Guard apply to a certain extent: there was no steady supply of uniforms, and makeshift outfits had to do. The important item they had to have was evidence that they were actively helping the war effort, so that white feathers for alleged cowardice could be avoided. The answer to that was that they wore a badge; gold escutcheon rimmed with red and stating, 'Grimsby and Cleethorpes VTC'.

Naturally, the young cadets were destined to enlist in various regiments, and so their training was methodical and professional: they were officially the Junior Company. It was a workable and successful system. The force may not have attracted the same media attention as the Chums, whose every movement seems to have been photographed and described, but they were vitally important to home security.

In April 1915, *The Grimsby News* printed details of the conditions of membership of the Volunteers, and there were a few fine details to explain, such as these strictures, which stressed that no shirkers were allowed:

> In recognising and permitting volunteer organizations the authorities have made a condition that no one of military age shall be enrolled unless he provides a valid excuse for not joining HM forces and even then he will be required to signify his consent to join if called upon to do so. ... It means simply that a man of military age cannot escape conscription if it is put in force by claiming to be a member of a Volunteer Training Corps.

Eligibility was made crystal clear: 'All able-bodied men who are thirty-eight years of age and upwards, who are medically or physically unfit for enlistment, or who can give valid reasons for not enlisting at once are eligible for membership.'

There was no delay or backwardness in openly appealing for men. A recruiting squad paraded every night at half-past seven, and the companies at both Grimsby and Cleethorpes took it in turns to operate the squad.

The young men who didn't walk around as soldiers must have been paranoid about receiving white feathers. Even the troops on the march were aware of these things, as this extract from an anonymous diary from late 1914 shows:

> June 17. Went for a route march and attended bathing parade. On the march the boys were very busy asking all the young chaps in the street why they weren't in khaki. Greengrocers threw fruit at us but they soon got tired of that.

In some places the rush to enlist met with frustration, so it was not always a matter of instantly becoming a soldier. This report from Yorkshire for instance, makes this clear: 'Some weeks ago three workmen from a large engineering works wished to join the "Pals" battalion which has been raised in Leeds ... a request came that they should not be proceeded with because their services were best required in their regular calling.'

It is also interesting and useful to note that in this war there was quite a degree of interaction between various regiments with regard to home defence. For instance, not far to the north, over into East Yorkshire and the coast, the 3rd Lancashire Fusiliers were charged with defending that coast and the Humber against invasion. Consequently, the volunteers around Grimsby and Immingham were close to an outfit that included a mix of men from all kinds of earlier war experience. Incidentally, one of the men with the Lancashires in 1917 was the writer J.R.R. Tolkien.

Every community in Britain was ready for the call to arms in 1914, and Grimsby was no exception. When Westminster looked to its greatest assets and resources, the major ports and industries were at the top of the list, and Grimsby was both: it had the commercially important fishing fleet and the communication network the fleet needed well in place. The town was destined to something very different from the war than was at first envisaged. Statements about the conflict 'being over by Christmas' were of course proved to be inaccurate, by a long way. During the first few months, it was clear to most people that the war was going to involve far more than two armies facing each other on the fields of Belgium and Northern France.

The German Schlieffen Plan entailed the assumption that if the army of the Reich formed a line on the Eastern Front, facing Russia, while also being established in France and moving through by the coast to take Belgium, then the Russian response would be so slow that a swift action in the western area would be over by the time there was anything to worry about over in the east. The plan involved Belgian neutrality being violated, and Britain was obliged to respond by helping her allies, France and Belgium. When people back home became aware of that, and when they read about atrocities on the Belgians allegedly being committed by German troops, there was a sense of growing magnitude of the war. State followed state, taking sides, and such a massive conflict needed huge resources. It needed, in short, a domestic supply route, the production of armaments in great quantities, and a gargantuan civilian effort back home to 'keep the home fires burning' in every sense, as Ivor Novello's song reminded people.

Very soon after war was declared, there were initiatives in place to help with resources and to support families. For instance, the Mayor's Relief Fund was started. The first reason for this was to provide food and some cash, but it became a massive general charity for the war effort, and well over £12,000 was given out in relief measures. There was also the Minesweepers' Fund, headed by Tom Sutcliffe. As an example of what was achieved, this extract from a summary of the work done will suffice:

In one week, 102 families (soldiers, sailors, dependents, fishermen's widows, old age pensioners) received groceries, coal or bread tickets; eighty-six women were helped at the Welfare Centres, with milk for nursing mothers and babies, and nourishment for expectant mothers.

There was also the YMCA, whose huts are to be seen on many an old photograph of the Western Front, and which figures in so many memoirs. But they were also busy at home: they presented concerts and, of course, provided hostels. They even used a temperance hotel, probably the hotel in Cleethorpes Road. At one time there were 158 beds created there.

In September there was a major fundraising and recruiting event, and a special publication, *The Flag*, was printed, with the mayor's supervision. The occasion was Union Jack Day, something that the mayor, Alderman J.H. Tate, relished, as it was, he claimed, a 'first' for his town:

Union Jack Day is an attempt to raise a sum of £500 towards the local contribution to the National Relief Fund. … There has been as yet no systematic attempt to secure the coppers of those, who, while anxious to help the good cause, are too modest to forward their small but none the less welcome donations. … The Union Jack Day originated in Grimsby but since it has been before the public it has been eagerly taken up in other quarters, and many larger, more important centres of industry are now organizing similar collections; indeed a suggestion has been put forward that Union Jack Day should be celebrated generally throughout the Empire on a date to be fixed.

The Flag gives us a very special insight into the mentality of the time with regard to fundraising and to recruitment of men to fight. The contents included a supposed story of 'Private Micky of the First Lincolns', in which a supposedly typical young man of the town 'finds himself' and his true qualities in military action. Micky is depicted as the kind of rebel who is liable to indiscipline and waywardness but who in the end is the salt of the earth in uniform. The story begins with an account of the man's failings:

Micky was a classic case of finding trouble. If he couldn't find it at first sight he hunted it up. It was generally accepted by his squadron that if the Recording Angel duly set down all the anathema uttered by the sergeant major upon Micky during the nine years he was in the service, the volume, inscribed 'Account of Private Michael Fotherby' was undoubtedly bulky.

Micky is stressed as having pluck and character, just waiting to be shaped to the desired end by army discipline: 'Once he came home to Grimsby on furlough he told his comrades on return that he "enjoyed himself all right",' and then we have: 'In his sober moments he would tell his mum that he was a kind of misfit.'

What was the fate of this 'misfit'? We might have guessed that it was heroism in the extreme. This is the account of his noble deed:

Then came the order to retreat, and Micky began to fall back with the rest; whilst doing so he saw his colonel stricken down by a stray bullet. Micky could have saved his life by continuing to retreat. That would not have been Micky's way. Without hesitation, he dashed back across the enemy's firing line, picked up the colonel and carried him on his back under the enemies' fire until he brought him safely into the Allies' ranks. On the way Micky was fatally wounded. He died twenty minutes after he had saved the colonel.

The ultimate moral message is that Micky meets the Recording Angel, and of course, the old book is discarded, and we have the quote: 'He that loseth his life shall find it.'

The Union Jack Day was a huge occasion. There was a negro minstrel band, and in tableaux performed by local people from all walks of life, the scenes included 'Nurses Tending Wounded Soldiers' and 'Join Kitchener's Army'. In costume, people dressed as Britannia, John Bull, an African Zulu, a Red Indian and Miss Dolly Roach. Miss Mollie Freeman dressed as India, and Miss Mary Buffery as New Zealand. The Grand Procession comprised more than 10,000 children, and everything was organized in the way that reflected the love of the order and discipline that had made the British a military race: 'The procession will be marshalled in two sections, which will unite at Riby Square, and leaving there at three o'clock promptly will proceed by the following route.' Another grand procession followed, in the evening, such was the stamina of the locals.

The booklet is peppered with miniature portraits of local men who were already fighting – as part of the British Expeditionary Force. The images show representatives from the whole spectrum of the military establishment, from W. Johnson of the 5th Lincolns to H.L. Mitchell of the 1st Coldstreams, who had fought at Mons. Of course, there was rousing verse as well, including these words from *Lines to Bill*:

Once there came a misty morn,
Kaiser Bill;
And they had to up and fight
With our Jacks who are brave and bright;
Well they showed you England's might,
Didn't they Bill?

Also very quick to respond to the call was the 'special' police force. All through British history, in times of public disorder or political turmoil, special police have been formed. Before the regular police appeared after 1829, the specials were rather marginal figures, alongside the militia, but by the early twentieth century they were well established. In Grimsby more than a thousand men joined the special police during the war years, and at its strongest it had manpower of about 770. When formed it was led by Major Bennett, and after his transfer to the armed forces, Captain Warner was at the helm, and then Calvin Wright was their Chief. As the 1919 publication on the war effort noted, 'Much of the work of the Specials lay in ordinary street duty, their presence enabling the Chief Constable (Mr John Stirling) to release forty-six men for the army, but on fifty-seven occasions air raid action has been taken.'

In Grimsby, the establishment figures wasted no time in writing and speaking about the need for fighting men. The Reverend Canon

Markham expressed a common attitude: 'If it be true that working men are ignorant of the necessity of the war and of the grave issues which hang on it, let me humbly suggest that the leaders of both the great political parties arrange press meetings at once and speak from the same platform.'

The Chums on the march in the town centre.
Lincolnshire Archives

The first step was, of course, to gather the Territorial forces. A photo from 1914 shows John Stirling, the chief constable of Grimsby for thirty years, inspecting and addressing lines of volunteers from that body of men. Only seven days after war was declared, Lord Kitchener had written to all the Lord Lieutenants of the shires, requesting the assembly

of the volunteer men. Kitchener's aim was to create a large number of what he thought of as 'Pals battalions' – so that workmates and neighbours would enlist together. This had happened before; since the threats from Napoleon more than a century earlier, the militia regiments had similarly gathered.

What was to become known as the Grimsby Chums battalion was the result. The origins of this celebrated force lie in the actions of some 'old boys' of the Municipal College, who contacted a man who was previously the head – Captain A.J. Stream. The college had had a cadet corps, and it was recognized that there was a company of soldiers in the making. Soon a small cadre of men were drilling, regardless of what else might emerge from their plans. There was a recruiting committee in the town as well – as there was everywhere in the land – and from a meeting on the subject of raising men, the result was that a company was offered to the 5th Lincolnshires. At the end of August, the *Grimsby Telegraph* announced that men were wanted for the 5th Lincolns: 'The commanding officer, Col Sandall, is very anxious to bring the battalion up to war strength before it leaves this country and Grimsby is required to do its share towards filling up the ranks.'

The recruiting for the 5th Lincolnshires was very active. On 30 August, not only was there a full-page appeal for '500 men from all classes' that 'must be recruited at once' but there was also a strongly worded account of the likely pool of local men and what the desired qualities in these Territorials might be, stressing that private soldiers were needed, not officers:

> There are a large number of young men in the town who, owing to their social position, have no doubt been looking forward to taking commissions, but we understand that there are already an ample number of officers, and that there are many on the waiting list. Whereas it takes only two or three months to teach a man to march and shoot, the necessary training for the position of officer could not be obtained in such a small space of time.

But the Chums were destined to be a force on their own, such was the continuing answer to the call. Numbers steadily grew, and on 9 September, the Chums were officially defined and created, being at that time the 10th battalion of the Lincolnshires.

It was to be a very long process of training and preparation; new soldiers could not simply be given uniforms and guns and taken to the front. For months there was drill and field training, escalating after the end of September when the strength reached 500 men. The Artillery

Barracks in Victoria Street became the HQ and companies were formed. Then, by October, Lieutenant Colonel Heneage became their official commanding officer.

The most significant step forward came when the Earl of Yarborough gave the Chums a site on his land at Brocklesby and a camp was built by J.R. Thompson, builders from Grimsby. But for several months there were no rifles or proper uniforms, as everything took time and had to be done through the proper channels. At least the men were in their huts by Christmas, and by then events had shown everyone that the war was intensifying – and in fact it was coming nearer to home. History has provided us with a full record of the Chums: lots of photos exist, perhaps the most telling ones being of the men on the move or at Brocklesby Park. One picture in particular gives a great deal of information: it shows them carrying kitbags and walking in line past Hewson Chapman's timber yard at Lock Hill. They wear civilian caps so they could be mistaken for tram conductors, and the kitbags are stunningly white.

Two young men pose in a studio shot – this was the most common memento for families to keep. *Author's collection*

The week before Christmas, as the Chums settled into their huts and began to feel like soldiers rather than civilians with wooden sticks, the Zeppelins came.

The Zeppelins were the German airships. They were rigid airships, designed by Count Ferdinand von Zeppelin. They had first taken to the air in 1900. One of the very early flights was witnessed by Stefan Zweig (an Austrian novelist and member of the Young Vienna group of important writers), who saw it being ripped from its moorings and whipped away – an inauspicious beginning for what would be a menace to Britain. Zweig wrote about the very first flight as well: 'I was on my way to Belgium and happened to be in Strasbourg where … it circled the

Some nervous looking young recruits to the Chums at Brocklesby.
Lincolnshire Archives

Munster. … That evening, news came that it had crashed in Echterdingen.'

As early as 6 August, Zeppelins had been used to bomb Liège. Now, between December 1914 and early 1916, there were Zeppelin raids and shelling from German cruisers. Three towns were attacked: Scarborough, Hartlepool and Whitby. There were heavy casualties; forty-four died and there were sixty-six injured. The very thought of these giant balloon-like monsters floating above England, and of battleships attacking property near the coast and bringing death and destruction on what was now becoming 'the home front' was terrifying. They were very difficult to approach at that time; the height they flew at meant that the planes could not intercept them, and also, they were out of the range of the ground-based anti-aircraft guns.

When such a horrendous thing happened, naturally there was an atmosphere of fear and panic, and also a flow of misinformation, scaremongering and apprehension. One rhyme that circulated then was:

Absolute evidence I have none –
But my aunt's charwoman's sister's son
Heard the policeman in Downing Street
Say to a housemaid on his beat
That he has a brother, who has a friend
Who knows the day when the war will end ...

One woman wrote in her diary: 'The raid night was horrid. I got E & S into a big building … every moment we expected to hear the bombs drop close by or on us, for the machines sounded overhead.'

There had never been attacks over the British mainland before like this. The heart of the massive British Empire was under threat from an enemy who came by air, not by sea. That fact alone was shocking. Obviously, the Yorkshire towns that had been hit were not so far from Grimsby. It all seemed too fearsome to contemplate. One press report read: 'At Scarborough three churches, hotels and many private houses were wrecked or damaged. Seventeen people were killed. At Whitby, sad to relate, the ruins of the famous old abbey were still further laid low. Two people were killed and two wounded.'

How were these monsters of the sky to be confronted? Very soon after

The men of the 1 and 2 platoons relaxing at Brocklesby Park during training. *Lincolnshire Archives*

Ships in the Royal Dock. Note the number of ships seen behind, at sea.
Grimsby Central Library

war broke out, there had been a Royal Naval Air Service base established at Skegness. There were Royal Navy fuel tanks at Immingham and so air patrols from Skegness went over that area. But common sense dictated that the base should be closer, and soon there was an Immingham base, known as RNAS Killingholme, and there were four planes there in late 1914.

Spy mania and the menacing thought of any aliens being hidden enemies began to capture the public's imagination. On 5 December the first German spy was shot in the Tower. 'He took his chances and lost the game,' *The Spectator* stated. Naturally, the ports were seen as vulnerable locations in that respect. To make matters worse, by the last months of 1914 there were Belgian refugees to consider. Heneage, the Chums' commander, wrote to *The Times* to explain the situation in his home area:

> General Nugent, commanding the coast defences on the Humber and to a point about 15 miles north of Grimsby, has ordered all aliens from Belgium to remove to a distance of 12 miles from the coast, but the local government board write and ask the Lindsey Relief Committee to arrange, without any restriction of area, for reception of Belgian refugees generally.

In other words, as Heneage summed up, 'All is perfect chaos.' To make matters worse, the magistrates were assuming that the orders carried out by Nugent were being done. The War Office, Admiralty and the Home Office, it seemed, were not talking to each other.

Heneage had put his finger on a hot topic of the time: the problem of 'aliens' from overseas. In times of war this was complex. After all, there would now be large numbers of Belgians wanting to scramble onto a ship and escape from the advancing armies of the Kaiser to settle under the protective wing of their British allies. There had been the Aliens Act of 1906, which placed inspectors at major ports, including Grimsby, but immigrants soon realised that if they journeyed in groups of less than forty, they would not be inspected. Then, as soon as war broke out, a new statute, the Aliens Restrictions Act, came into force. This led to German-owned enterprises of all kinds being confiscated, and consequently to an increase in anti-German feeling generally. Matters were tightened up. The police handbook, issued by the chief constable of Lincolnshire, had this paragraph, which stayed in force until after the war:

> No alien coming from outside the United Kingdom shall land except with the leave of the Immigration Officers. There are many restrictions and certain ports to land at which do not concern the

police, but it is the duty of the police to render assistance to an Immigration Officer as far as possible and if requested by such Officer to take into custody and institute proceedings in respect of any alien detained by an Immigration Officer.

One of the most large-scale preparations for war was the development of the trawlers, as they were adapted for action against the enemy fleet. In 1907 the Admiral Lord Charles Beresford had been to Grimsby to watch some trawlers undergo trials. The vessels swept some dummy 'mines', and the admiral was impressed. In fact, he was so impressed that in 1914, when England faced the dismal prospect of having to cope with German submarines, no less than 156 Grimsby trawlers were initially taken to be converted into minesweepers. Beresford had conducted negotiations in 1911 to make sure that the Admiralty and trawler owners could work together to make sure that if there was a war, the designated trawlers would be converted to do minesweeping patrols. This means that there was already a Trawler Section of the Royal Naval Reserve (RNR) when war broke out. There was a taut, specific agreement between the Admiralty and the parties involved, including a valuation of ships at £18 for each ton of gross tonnage and £40 for each defined unit of horsepower.

But what is an agreement in times of peace is very different from what happens in war. Gradually, it became clear that the Admiralty could requisition vessels, and it took an agreement sorted out by the Ministry of Agriculture and Fisheries to placate the Grimsby men. One result was that the expertise of trawlermen was not necessarily fully used as the war began and developed. Journalist Robb Robertson has put it this way: 'In the event, the opportunity to make the most effective use of the fishing industry's fine pool of skilled labour was sadly missed, partly through inadequate official forethought and partly through the air of patriotic euphoria.'

Officially, the sweeping was undertaken by what became known as the National Auxiliary Patrol, a part of the RNR. Of course, fishing still had to continue, but as this was in addition to the minesweeping work, being a Grimsby fisherman was an extremely dangerous occupation in 1914. It did not take long for the casualty lists to appear in the press. The *Grimsby Telegraph* began to report on losses. After only a month of hostilities, there were twelve trawlers lost. One of the most dramatic stories in this early campaign was the destruction of the *Kilmarnock*, which was snapped in two and sunk. A historian writing in the 1920s said that 'it was more dangerous to be a Grimsby trawlerman than to be in the army' at that time. Facts supported this claim: the Admiralty announced in early September that the *Imperialist* had been the latest trawler casualty, noting that the ship had been blown up off the Tyne and that the ten survivors had been picked up by the *Rhodesian* of Scarborough. The *Reviso* hit a mine and sank in ten minutes, with the crew taken as prisoners, doomed to sit out the war as prisoners of the Reich. The Admiralty listed ten other trawlers lost in the previous month.

At the end of August, the papers reported losses in more detail. One feature explained the nature of the horror: 'The danger to shipping from mines laid in the North Sea, in contravention of the Hague Convention, continues to be manifested. … There is said to be little doubt that German vessels disguised as trawlers or neutral traders are laying mines.' The message to the public was clear: there was going to be nothing gentlemanly about this war.

The war had been in process only three weeks when one paper announced: 'Warnings have been issued at Grimsby that mines have been exploded by a herring drifter off the outer Dowsing buoy and others have been found 30 miles from the Tyne breakwater.' This referred to the Inner Dowsing lightship, which had been in place in the Humber estuary since 1861.

One establishment that was to be crucially important in the war was more than ready for action: the Railway Executive Committee, which had been created in 1912. This sprang from the War Railway Council of 1896, which had considered the establishment of railway services in support of wars overseas as well as at home. Railway historian George Dow, writing on this service, noted, 'Upon the Great Central the impact of war was immediate. Three of its steamships, *Bury*, *City of Bradford* and *City of Leeds*, were seized by the Germans.' This reminds us that the great railway companies were developing a reach and influence well beyond the home railway tracks.

Simon Batchelor, in a blog from the National Railway Museum, explained the situation and the consequences of the capture of the crews:

Initially it appears that the crews were interned aboard their vessels and the captains of the ships were allowed ashore to purchase supplies, but as the mood of the German populace changed they were confined with their crews. Both the Great Central Railways and the Lincolnshire and Yorkshire had agencies in Hamburg and subsequently supplies were purchased through them. The crews were visited by the American Consul and through his intervention the three female stewards were repatriated, arriving back in Grimsby on 24 September.

What happened after that was that the port of Immingham, just a few

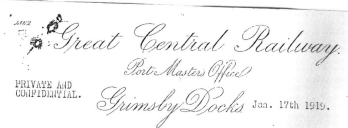

PRIVATE AND
CONFIDENTIAL.

Great Central Railway.
Port Masters Office
Grimsby Docks Jan. 17th 1919.

My Dear Sir,

I beg to submit herewith my report on the administration of Immingham and Grimsby Docks during the period of the War 1914 - 1918.

I feel that my report does not do justice to the services the Great Central Railway Coy. have rendered to the National requirements of this great War.

Many services, which at the time rendered were of considerable value and importance, have become dwarfed or forgotten in the lapse of time and succession of greater events, and the report does not disclose the many difficulties which have had to be overcome in order to arrive at the results achieved.

Immediately following the declaration of War, the Humber, and particularly Immingham and Grimsby Docks were absorbed as Naval Bases, and as Fleets arrived without knowledge of local facilities and conditions, they were in a great degree dependent upon myself and my staff for the provision of such facilities and general assistance.

When the Admiral of Patrols assumed command of this area, and as Competent Naval Authority exercised his powers under the Defence of the Realm Regulations, the position of dependence of the individual units upon myself and staff naturally diminished.

Similarly on the outbreak of War, Grimsby became a Military defensive position, and thousands of troops were moved in who were dependent upon the Great Central Railway Company to provide them with billets and accommodation.

This needless to say threw a very heavy strain upon our resources, as warehouses had to be cleared and lighting and sanitary arrangements provided.

I am sure you will readily appreciate the anxiety and responsibility of the position, for at that moment there were no regulations under a Competent Authority in operation, and emergencies arose where immediate action had to be taken and where I had no opportunity to obtain your authority.

The outstanding feature during the period covered by my report has been the smoothness with which the

Part of a post-war report written by Sam Fay concerning the Great Central Railway's participation in the war effort. *Author's collection*

miles along the coast from Grimsby, was developed into a major centre of operations. It was not only a mobilization centre for the West Riding Territorial Regiment in the first month of the war, as the Chums were still trying to assemble, it was also the headquarters of the Admiral of Patrols. A huge amount of coal was stored there also, and there were links with the burgeoning air force too, when some Humber ferries underwent conversion to seaplane carriers. Dow estimates that 'in the first six months of the war no less than 3,778 men, equal to 11% of the staff [of the railway] joined the armed forces.'

When a report was written at the end of the war, on the part played by the Great Central Railway, the author pointed out:

> On the outbreak of war, Grimsby became a military defensive position, and thousands of troops were moved in who were dependent on the Great Central Railway Company to provide them with billets and accommodation. This, needless to say, threw a very heavy strain upon our resources, as warehouses had to be cleared and lighting and sanitary arrangements provided.

The author of the report, Sir Sam Fay, pointed out what was arguably the most massive and disruptive imposition made on the town in 1914:

> The heaviest responsibility has been the accommodation of HM vessels … in fact the use made by the Admiralty of Immingham and Grimsby Docks has amounted to an unrestricted use of the Docks as if they were a naval dockyard, whilst at the same time the administration has been carried out entirely by the civil element.

The tone of the report, and the inferences the reader has to make, reading between the lines, suggest that the adjustments ready for war imposed on Grimsby and Immingham were so great that they almost caused cracks at the seams – that it was a close-run affair.

On 19 October there was the first Battle of Ypres, and this led to the first German effort towards attacking British ports. In September there had been the battles of the Aisne and Marne. This early phase of the war has become known as 'the race to the sea' because the coastal area of Flanders was strategically very important: Germany was aiming at capturing the vitally useful ports of Dunkirk, Calais and Boulogne. The German Sixth Army was heading the attack here, and by the end of the year, the campaign ended with the First Battle Ypres. If the Germans lost this, then the Allies could enter Flanders, which had no geographical barriers to further advances. If the Germans should be victorious, they could have descended on those ports with a great advantage.

The British were essentially the British Expeditionary Force, the first professional British army across the channel. This was composed of 70,000 regular troops with additional reservist groups. These are the men who became known as the 'Contemptibles' because the Kaiser had called them a 'contemptible little army'. The fight at Ypres had almost obliterated the professional army, and from then onwards, there was to be a reliance on the volunteer forces. The other real consequence of that terrible confrontation was that the necessity of trench-based combat became a hard fact.

It became clear that the notion of the war 'ending by Christmas' was nonsense. We might gain some idea of the scale of the confrontation as at the opening of the war in August when we note that Germany had 1,077 battalions in the field, and the Allies had 1,632 battalions. The early death toll was staggering: 6,427 Belgian and French civilians had been killed in 1914, and there had been the outrage of Dinant as well – the town in Belgium where more than 600 people were shot dead by the German army on 23 August. The infamous 'Belgian

Two brothers, or perhaps brothers in arms, just before enlistment.
Author's collection

atrocities' were documented, and of course they were exaggerated as the propaganda war advanced, but there was a horrendous truth at the core of the story.

On September 4, the *Daily Mail* gave some shocking statistics on their front page, with the announcement '10,345 now killed, wounded or missing'. They added, 'War – as ever – comes hardest on the women. Full hearts make mute tongues, but some women draw together. Heaven perhaps listens to what they say of the sceptre author of the agonies of all the humble of Europe.'

On the home front, support work intensified and spread into all kinds of factory production. One factory worker described the situation: 'We make the khaki kitbags, the beds and pillows, aeroplane covers and tents etc. … Perhaps it is the drab colour of the khaki that reminds us so vividly of the brave lads who sooner or later must don it.' Naturally, there was an uneasy and unnerving atmosphere in and around Grimsby in those last months of the year. On 3 November the North Sea was officially labelled a 'military area', which meant that all vessels crossing the sea would be stopped and searched by Royal Navy ships. This is a reminder that the German civilians had a tough time as well; this was part of a strategy to create food shortages, and it was partially successful.

Everyone was doing their bit. The Cleethorpes ladies were reported by the *Grimsby Telegraph* as having produced 'no fewer than 527 articles for the use of our soldiers' and these included '163 shirts, 190 pairs of socks, 33 cardigan jackets', and '£25 in cash has been subscribed.' The National Relief Fund was up and running by the end of August as well, with local individuals and firms having donated the huge sum of £5,923 by the end of the month.

The advertising for the Relief Fund was dynamic to say the least. There were appeals with pictures of Tommies amidst bombs, bayonets out and ready for the scrap, with the words 'Doing his bit – Do Yours today!' The appeals were worded usually like an exhortatory lecture: 'The nation is not putting down the cash. The Relief Fund ought to have £20,000,000 by now. There are hundreds of men and women in Grimsby who can easily afford a sovereign each who have not given a penny.'

There was humour as well, such as this comic letter to 'The Emperor':

Regret to report, couldn't find entrance to fish dock. Some Boy Scouts on lock-pit. Retired in good order with ship's band playing *Deutschland über alles.*

Von Turpentine

Since the early losses of the trawlers *Tubal Cain* and *Fittonia* in August, it was clear that death had come to Grimsby families: the threat was there, with seven men lost from the *Fittonia*. We have a substantial knowledge of the *Tubal Cain*, because it had left Grimsby before war was declared and the men taken on board the *Kaiser Wilhelm der Grosse*, and then the skipper kept a diary, and he wrote an account of the events. He stated, 'When we were all nicely on board they fired on our ship and put forty-five shots in her. One of the officers came to me, saying, "She is British. She takes a lot of sinking" … We lived well and were treated with the best of respect.'

The *Grimsby Telegraph* reported, 'It is believed that they [the crew] are on their way on board the SS *Manda*. … The skipper of the lost vessel is Captain William Smith of Legsby Avenue.' The situation provoked a hostile response from the Royal Navy of course: The *Grimsby Telegraph* of 30 August carried this message from the Admiralty, making it clear that they had not killed any of their own:

> Having regard to the great injuries which are being inflicted on neutral vessels by mines in the North Sea, it should be clearly understood that while the Admiralty reserves itself the right to adopt … retaliatory measures … it has not up to the present laid a single mine, and is therefore not chargeable with any injuries up to the present.

But of course, along with the misery of war comes the paradox of economic success. For instance, the firm of J.S. Doig doubled the number of men employed as they erected boiler shops, developing the fitting shop and machinery, and they broadcast the fact that they were 'now in a position to take work of any description'.

The recruiting fever continued through the last months of 1914. In the *St James' Magazine* for October, the vicar wrote in his parochial letter:

> On Sunday, 20 October the battalion attended divine service, about 400 strong … most gladdening to see the fine type of young fellows who have been attracted to the ranks. Bank clerks, businessmen, all in a good position and earning good salaries, and voluntarily leaving everything in obedience to the country's call.
> … There can be little doubt that the required 1,100 will be forthcoming, if only our young fellows put their backs into it and come forward and urge others to do the like.

The mindset everywhere was for men to heed the call and enlist. After another year had passed, the men in the trenches would be singing such ditties as *Send my mother/send my sister and my brother/but for Gawd's sake don't send me*. But in the autumn of 1914, such was the fervour for young men to take the khaki and join up that fake telegrams were sent to homes whose men were still in civvies, addressed to 'Mrs I. Stoppham' or to 'Mr Will Keepham' pointing out such sentiments as 'You appear to be happy for myself to answer the call on behalf of both your men'. Propaganda films showed soldiers writing letters from the front with notes such as 'Dear little woman, I hope you are keeping in top order, as I am, and that the kiddies are well' – emphasising the masculine toughness and willingness to sacrifice life and/or career to the good cause.

But the 'young fellows' that the vicar wanted to enlist had indeed done so, in great numbers. The Old Humberstonians roll of honour provided a regular listing of men on active service, and their lists show the range of regiments to which Grimsby men had gone to join up – outfits from the Lancashires to the Cheshires and from the East Yorkshire Yeomanry to the Leicester Regiment. The Chums were not yet at the front of course, but the first casualties started to be mentioned, such as Lieutenant Colonel Bell of the Bedfordshire Regiment, who died on 18 October. He had been in the ranks for over four years and had then gained a commission. His family were from Deansgate, Grimsby. The editorial continued the practice of mixing accounts of deaths, men missing and awards won, along with patriotic verses and rhetorical statements about the need for the good fight to continue, as in this, from the end of 1915:

> Nobly do Old Boys continue to do their part, and the Roll of Honour grows apace. Once again, I would ask all who can help by giving me information or corrections. … Another Old School Captain, Lieut L. Falkner, was reported missing on September 25th, and I regret to say that up to the present nothing more has been reported. He will be remembered by many Old Boys as a popular Captain, good at cricket, tennis and football. We hope to hear later of his safety.

Of course, the women were equally resilient and determined. They were ready to do whatever hard work was put their way. The popular view regarding women in Britain throughout the Victorian and Edwardian years was that they were markedly fragile, very much the weaker sex. The popular medical handbooks by Lydia Pinkham (the original of the song *Lily the Pink*) maintained that 'women who work' were particularly vulnerable to the effects of overwork: 'Women who must earn their living by sheer hard work have always cause to dread the period of menstruation. Nature cries out for them to rest, to lie down, to refrain from all exertion and excitement. The wheels of industry grind slowly on, allowing no respite or freedom.' Little did Lydia know what demands were about to be made on the female workforce. By the first months of 1915 women would be working very long hours, and doing men's work. But Lydia was right about the female resilience: she wrote, with regard to shop girls, 'who for long hours have to stand behind a counter, with ever a smile upon her face, no matter how great her suffering, with many a disagreeable customer to serve.' The war was to make that child's play, compared to driving huge vehicles, welding and handling explosives.

The year ended with horrific statistics of death from across the Channel, and with the beginnings of the war involving the trawlers in the North Sea. But as yet the recruits in the ranks of the Grimsby Chums were still in training at home. Few would have envisaged, that Christmas, what the future scale of that dreadful war was destined to be.

Chapter Two

1915: Deepening Conflict

Early in the new year, there was the triumph of the Battle of the Dogger Bank to offer some cheer to the nation. This was on 24 January, and as a code book had been taken, movements of German ships were known. British ships fell upon the German cruiser squadron and won a victory, with 950 German dead, as opposed to only fifteen British casualties.

For Grimsby though, the new year began with more bad news from the fight at sea. The steam trawler *Windsor*, from Grimsby, was adrift, and spotted by the *Bernicia*. On board was Skipper Harrison with eight men, and they had been drifting for a full day after the vessel had hit a mine. The remaining crew of the *Windsor* had been floating on the dangerously maimed vessel. The story was that they had hauled the trawl and brought the gear in when they hit a mine. One press report noted, 'The winch was stopped and it was then seen that one of the detonators of the mine was actually resting on the rail.' As the men had floated away, they could have been blown to high heaven at any time. The crew were shattered, and had seen the hull of their ship severely damaged. Thankfully, they were brought home.

This was the first phase of an intensification of the minesweeping and submarine war. By 20 April, one headline said it all: 'Murder by Torpedo: the killing of fisher folk'. This was prompted by the sinking of the trawler *Vanilla*, by a submarine, and after that attack, another trawler, the *Formo*, had been chased by a German sub for four hours. The skipper of the *Formo* gave an account:

> We were steaming slowly with our gear down, and the *Vanilla* was less than a quarter of a mile away ... there was a terrific explosion and we saw the *Vanilla* fly into the air in fragments. ... I ordered out our lifeboat ... but we had barely got the boat out when another submarine came up almost alongside of us, so near I could have thrown a biscuit aboard. I manoeuvred and she manoeuvred and then she discharged a torpedo. There was nothing to do but cut and run for it.

The skipper kept dodging, and finally, as night fell, they eluded the enemy.

The *Lullington* – one of the many vessels torpedoed off the east coast.
Author's collection

The next month was even worse. On 4 May the Grimsby trawler *Collingwood* found itself facing a submarine, and the crew decided to try to 'run for it'. It was destined to be sunk, along with no less than six ships from Hull that were out at sea that fateful day.

Of course, large numbers of Grimsby trawlermen were consequently taken as prisoners of war. When war had first been declared, there had been vessels in port in Germany, and there had been immediate captives taken. An Interned Prisoners' Relief Fund was started, and the men were certainly not forgotten. Some of them had been employees of the Great Central Railway as that company owned ships, and some of their own fleet were taken. The fishermen prisoners were not forgotten either: from 1914 to the end of 1918, about 33,000 food parcels were sent to them, along with 1,697 parcels of clothing. This had initially been organized by Miss Newnham, working with the Royal National Mission to Deep Sea Fishermen, which had been founded by Ebenezer Mather in 1881.

Reports of trawlers lost and missing came regularly, a typical piece being this, in which the list of crew members was attached:

After an absence of four months, during which time nothing has been heard of them, hope for the safety of the trawlers *Oxford* and

Lord Howick has at last been abandoned. Nothing has been heard of either vessels or their crew since the second week of September [1914], so it has been presumed that they have foundered with all hands.

There followed a melancholy listing of men missing: the *Oxford* had nine hands and the *Lord Howick* had ten.

With such a high rate of losses among the seamen, there was a desperate need for help, and for funds to support the men's families. A letter to the *The Grimsby News* from Isaac Miller, the Honorary Agent of the Shipwrecked Fishermen and Mariners' Society, stresses the urgency of the appeal:

Sir,

The above Society … had been assisting and will further help, the widows, orphans and other dependent relatives of fishermen and sailors losing their lives through explosion of German mines in the North Sea. The total amount expended in direct consequence of the war up to December 31st 1914 is £2,533 14s, affording relief to 152 widows, 289 orphans, 39 aged parents and 801 sailors and fishermen. I regret to say that Grimsby has had cause to make heavy demands on the Society's funds. About £400 of the above sum has come to Grimsby.

One of the most notable events of this period was the grounding of the submarine E13 on 17 August. Fifteen crew men died, and one was Herbert Staples, whose death was a prompt for *The Telegraph* to lament and celebrate at the same time – saying farewell to a man who died nobly, but celebrating the fact that Grimsby had another hero to be proud of. The account in *The Telegraph* had this section, which captures the defiant mood of Grimsby people:

And when the body was landed at the port this afternoon, and carried through the streets to its last resting place, the public showed, as we think it has never shown before, the depth of its sorrow, its respect and its admiration for its hero. … Perhaps, too, there was many a grim, silent resolve to be avenged for what, after all, was the result of one of the blackest crimes that an unscrupulous nation could commit.

Out at sea, in the estuary, there were also the gun batteries to think of. By the first months of 1915, the Stallingborough and Sunk Island units were beginning to take action, and as naval historian Jeffrey Dorman has written, 'This was a vital safeguard for any large normal or

A disturbing image of a Zeppelin over the docks. *Grimsby Central Library*

commercial port during wartime and its function is summed up by the
Fire Commander's Standing Orders: "To identify and ascertain the
character and intention of vessels seeking entry to the port and to ensure
adequate warning of the defences in the chance of suspicious or
unfriendly vessels entering the port."'

It was established that all shipping wanting to come to port would
have to know prearranged signals and show the right flags at designated
times; the signals and flags were changed, in the same way that codes are
constantly shuffled in war.

It is not at all surprising that, in this atmosphere, together with the
memory of the Zeppelins up the coast, the possibility of invasion was in
the air. Emergency measures were circulated: what should one do if there
were such a thing as an invasion? The Emergency Committees spelled
it out, with advice such as: 'Inhabitants of houses should go into the
cellars or lower rooms. If the houses are on a sea front, where they are

exposed to direct fire from the sea, the inhabitants should leave by the back door and seek shelter elsewhere.' It all seems a bit vague to the modern reader, and of course, terrifying. Other advice was naive, giving notes on behaviour that no human being would be able to keep to, such as: 'Gathering into crowds or watching the bombardment from an exposed position may lead to unnecessary loss of life.'

The minefield danger was truly frightening, and stories of danger and risk abounded. One of the most remarkable was the experience of Skipper George Laming, who found himself in the dock before the magistrate in April for running a vessel through the Humber without a pilot. He was prosecuted under the 1914 Defence of the Realm Act, which had the power to issue regulations to secure the navigation of vessels under the control of the Admiralty.

Laming had come in on Christmas morning, and he had been stopped by an examination ship. The crime report summarises:

> He told the officer he thought he knew the way through the mine fields without a pilot … and under the circumstances he risked it.
> … There was not only a danger to his crew in passing through the

Some civilians find a beached torpedo. *Author's collection*

mine field, but the fact that if one trawler attempted to do so it might endanger others it would encourage to come through.

The year 1915 also saw the development of the War Emergency Programme, which addressed the need for new batteries to be in place at Kilnsea and at Spurn Head. There were also the Humber forts to consider: these were at Bull Sand and Haile Sand, the latter being south of the Tetney Haven, and stretching down to a spot south of Donna Nook. The reason for this thinking was that there had been aggressive actions by the German fleet in the last months of 1914, when cruisers had attacked Yarmouth. Obviously, that long stretch of the Lincolnshire coast stretching up from Boston was vulnerable.

An interesting note about the naval centres close to Grimsby is that, just a few years before the war, Immingham almost became a major base for the Royal Navy. An anonymous writer for the *Grimsby Telegraph* wrote a feature about a Finance Committee meeting at Immingham in 1909 and a plan for a new dock emerged. The secretary of the Humber Graving and Engineering Company composed a letter stating that Admiralty requirements would be met and that a subsidy of £48,000 a year for thirty years would be needed. As the writer concludes: 'In a letter dated June 12 1909 the secretary of the Admiralty wrote, "I am commissioned by my Lords of the Admiralty to express their thanks to the directors … for the detailed proposals … my Lords regret that the large liabilities which they would have to incur make it impossible to adopt the scheme."' And the writer adds, 'Had the scheme been adopted by the Admiralty there may well have been a naval dockyard at Immingham.'

There was also an intensifying climate of fear and paranoia about spies and the need for secrecy. What has been called 'Spy mania' was setting in. This rhyme, which went the rounds, sums up part of the attitude:

A wise old owl lived in an oak.
The more he heard the less he spoke;
The less he spoke the more he heard.
Why aren't we all like that wise old bird?

But there was no denying that Grimsby had its spies. In this atmosphere, Grimsby had its episode of spy activity. A Swede called Ernst Olsson was convicted at Lincoln Assizes on 17 June 1915 of trying to gather information that would constitute an offence under the Official Secrets Act of 1911. The Act and all its provisions sprang from years of uncertainty about how to change and streamline the military intelligence of the realm. After the Boer War of 1899–1902 and the dynamic growth of the German Empire in Africa, Britain was confused about how to plan and improve its actions against espionage at home. The German intelligence system, initially naval with Admiral von Tirpitz in charge, was certainly organizing a spy ring here, and the new MI5 department under Colonel Vernon Kell had been impressively effective against these spies who were looking for information at dockyards.

Every sea port was vulnerable and Grimsby was no exception. Olsson was charged with looking for information about the defences and sea power elements as observed in the Humber. Another Swede who was living in Grimsby, Erander, had been working with him. On 16 March a conversation between these two had been overheard and reported. In this interchange they said that in the coming war the Germans were sure to win and Olsson started to talk about some German friends in Rotterdam. He said that they were trying to extract some information about the naval and military situation in Grimsby. He was heard asking Erander for that type of information. They were being tailed and clearly it was not difficult to listen in on their talk, because a week later they were listened to again and this time Erander was asked if he had made a decision about passing on such information. Erander's actual words were noted. He said, 'Life is sweeter than money to me; I have been in Grimsby fifteen years and I have been treated like a man, and it would be the last thing I should do.'

That second conversation was the foundation of the accusation against Olsson; he had said that some of his friends were Germans, and as a German fleet was poised for action at Rotterdam he was condemned. On 7 April they met again and he repeated that statement. He said that his friends over the North Sea were working hard to obtain the military information. Then, stepping up the talk to something more definite and alarming, he spoke of a fleet of 130 or 170 Zeppelins that were ready to fly over the sea to drop bombs on England when the weather was right. When the talkative Swede actually moved on to talk about him being a U-boat pilot he was really in trouble. After that Olsson wandered into *Boy's Own* territory, with a discourse about him being set up in a small boat on the east coast 'with petrol and provisions to supply the Germans at sea'.

Lipson Ward, defending the Swede, managed to argue that last statement away, defining it as irrelevant to the charge. At his appeal hearing in February, that last statement was successfully removed as indictable, but the second ground for appeal – that the trial had been prejudiced by a card found on his person – was judged to be admissible. The card had been a summary of naval signalling, something that it was argued was generally available and he had owned since 1911.

The judge, Mr Justice Horridge, allowed the charge about the card to stand and the Swede was cross-examined. Everything the defence could come up with failed: Olsson was sentenced to four years' penal servitude. The Official Secrets Act – something people were still trying to fully understand – had clearly laid down that penal servitude was the punishment for 'communicating or intending to communicate secrets to a foreign state or an agent of a foreign state'. Olsson's talk of friends in Rotterdam had been his downfall.

In the same year, a certain Carl Muller had been executed by firing squad for spying; he also had friends in Rotterdam and he had sent letters to them written in German, about shipping dispositions. Robert Rosenthal met the same fate after sending coded details to Germany about shipping in Hull.

The efficiency of the team of officers led by Kell in London was astonishing, and it stemmed from an overheard conversation on a train in which two Germans were discussing a letter from Potsdam about British preparations for war. Grimsby played its part in that successful counter-espionage ring and the detectives busy at the port were part of a team working at all major ports. As far as Olsson was concerned, there seems to have been an element of fantasy and wish-fulfilment in his ramblings to his friend. In fact, the words spoken by his friend are very important in understanding the depth of support for counter-espionage among civilians: after all, Erander had been welcomed and respected in his adopted country and this was a buffer against the blandishments of his friend, who was convinced of German superiority.

As a writer to the paper had said in the same year, discussing the German spy scares, 'Altogether different is the position of the spy in time of peace. In some cases he is merely an adventurer working for money; he is then corrupt and it is his business to corrupt others.' That is exactly what Olsson was trying to do, but he was too bold and careless. He never would have made a James Bond. But there was a larger scale development well into operation: the spymasters in Germany had in fact organized a widespread operation. In 1907, a man called Widenmann had taken over as naval attaché in England, and he had three agents ready and waiting to serve him.

One of these agents managed to start an association linking his work with a company called the Argo Steamship Company, who were based in Bremen. The agent, de Boer, would act as the agent in Hull and Grimsby, working for the organization in Germany running espionage, the Admiralstab. The plan didn't really work and de Boer was neglected by his masters for some time.

In May 1915, the great Cunard liner RMS *Lusitania*, which had set sail from New York on 1 May, was hit by a torpedo from a German U-boat off the coast of Southern Ireland. There was much anti-German feeling across the country, and in Grimsby a few months before that disaster, there had been trouble at Fred Schwind's pork butcher's shop. The *Hull Daily Mail* reported on 9 June:

> The sinking of Grimsby trawlers and the deaths of inoffensive Grimsby fishermen resulted in expressions of indignation in Grimsby. So much so that Mr Schwind's pork butcher's shop and Mr Moller's shops on Albert Street, Cleethorpes Road and Hainton Avenue, were victims. Mr Schwind and Mr Moller were both naturalized. Mr Schwind in 1897. … The trouble was caused by women who assembled outside the shops and started to throw stones which first cracked and then broke the plate glass.

There had been anti-German feeling since the outbreak of war, of course, as there was everywhere. As Peter Chapman (historian of the Grimsby Chums) has written about William Hitzen, German Consul in Grimsby since 1877, even such a familiar naturalized German could be a scapegoat: 'Within a day or two of 4 August 1914, red paint was thrown at the front door. Hitzen, now sixty-six, became ill. A short stay in Bournemouth did nothing to help and he returned home to die in January 1915.'

At the beginning of 1915 it had become clear that the war was on a far grander and almost incomprehensible scale than anyone had imagined when the conflict began. What was also clear was that it would now be an effort involving everyone – men, women and children. Everyone had a part to play. Women, in particular, would be called upon to engage in all kinds of industrial work. Across the land, there were already a large number of trades that were carried out in small premises as family businesses, and women were involved in this, as is shown by the amazingly productive soldering and metal trade in Birmingham, for instance, where 'Grandma Page's factory' – a shed behind a house – was the place where a huge number of badges were made. The Great War certainly created a massive demand for such things. One woman, when interviewed on the trade, said, 'they made all the military badges.'

That involvement of women in war-based production was to become a major element in Grimsby's war work, and as W.H. Scott (author of a massive survey of the Yorkshire home front experience) wrote in 1923, 'Men everywhere were being released from industry and women were taking their places on the tramways and railways, in offices and workshops.' The problems came with the advent of what has become known as the munitions crisis. By the first few months of the year, it

was evident that there was a shortage of what were called 'munitions', which basically meant any hardware relating to weaponry. The shell crisis made things happen. Lloyd George, Minister of Munitions, which office had been created in May, said, 'It is a war of munitions. We are fighting against the best organized community in the world, the best organized either for peace or war.' A Lincolnshire man, Christopher

Here we see very clearly how capably women take over the demanding physical tasks normally in men's daily labour.
Courtesy of Grimsby Central Library, North Lincolnshire Libraries

Addison, was in charge of national supply channels, and he developed the rationale of 'War Socialism'. This entailed evolving a whole concept of production, with an eye on economy and efficiency, and also a sense of production targets.

But to a certain extent, life at home had to go on with the usual sport and recreation. In fact, given the long and tiring work being done by people of all ages, there was all the more need for entertainment and distraction. It had been assumed at the beginning of the war that there would be just a brief period of disruption to cultural and sporting matters and then all would be well. But, as may be seen in the case of Grimsby

Another powerful image showing the women of Grimsby doing men's work.
Grimsby Central Library

Town FC, although they started positively, the effects of the loss of team members had an impact, and after a poor season it was reluctantly decided that full-time football could not be maintained. The professional nature of the game was on hold and the major challenge cups were cancelled after the 1914–15 season.

The authors of the standard history of Grimsby Town comment on the war years with a tone of flatness and sometimes despair, particularly when it has to be noted that in the 1917–18 season they lost one match to Bradford 9–0 (although they were playing without a proper goalkeeper).

The stage still went on entertaining. In January 1915, for instance, at the Prince of Wales Theatre the locals went to see *Brewster's Millions*, and the review celebrated the production in joyful terms: 'Miss Emma Hutchinson and Mr Perry Hutchinson are making a most welcome reappearance in *Brewster's Millions*, the prosperity of which is undoubtedly as great ... as when first produced in Grimsby nine years ago.'

At The Palace, the established variety turns went on, feeding the love of a good song and plenty of comedy that had defined the stage in Edwardian times, and which still held its own against the movies. The stars were Miss Zena Vevey and Mr Max Erard. Zena was lauded as 'undoubtedly one of the most charming and expressive singers of ballads and high-class sentimental songs at present appearing on the music-hall stage'. In support were many other performers, including Campbell and Scott, novelty trapeze artistes, Billy Camp (a 'smart, burlesque character comedian') and Josie, a 'dainty Dutch comedienne and dancer'.

A scene showing the interior of the shell factory in Victoria Street. The premises were previously used for fish curing.
Grimsby Central Library

The picture shows the sheer efficiency of the loading and transport process as the shells begin their journey to the trenches on these munitions wagons. *Grimsby Central Library*

formed and premises were rented from Alec Black (later to be knighted) and the Chair was Councillor J.W. Eason, who was the mayor at the time. Jackson notes, 'The Board purchased the whole of the machinery on behalf of the Ministry, and work began in November, 1915.' But there was planning long before that. The building was first taken over in July, and in that month The Munitions and Light Castings Co of Granville Street, who were making Mills bombs, were ready to install more machinery. The rent was fixed and a light railway agreed, to operate from Knott and Barker's timber yard. Then, in August, a group of men were taught how to make shells.

Tenders were put out for blinds or curtains for the factory, which was to be in Victoria Street. On 21 August, extra lathes were ordered and wages were worked out. The blinds were agreed on by early September, and then the main task was to find a manager and to arrange for the place to be guarded. On 10 October the Volunteer Training Corps were taken on as guards and all that remained was to find the manager – and they found Mr F.H. Fleming, who turned out to be the ideal man for the job. After the war, Jackson wrote to Mr Doig, from whose firm Fleming had been borrowed: 'Dear Mr Doig, we have come to the end of our labours. … Thanks for the loan to this factory of the services of Mr Fleming, first as draughtsman and then as Works Manager.'

At one point, the factory employed more than 600 people. As one contemporary booklet comments: 'The operation of the Grimsby shell works was characterized by very good relations between the management and their employees and the plant was regarded as being one of the most efficient in Britain.'

The Chums were still in training in 1915. In June they had moved from Brocklesby Park to Ripon, where they encamped at Studley Royal. They were now officially the 101st Infantry Brigade of the 34th Division, along with contingents of Royal Scots and Suffolks. From there they were taken to Perham Down at Salisbury Plain, where their experience was dour and unpleasant compared to their earlier training. As part of Kitchener's New Army, they were destined to see action the following year, but for the moment they were to stay at Perham, and that period of preparation lasted through until early January 1916.

Over the sea, on the Western Front, those Grimsby men who had joined other regiments or who were already soldiers when war had broken out were learning hard lessons about the kind of war they had entered. It was now a case of attrition, of steady, slow and costly advances over the vast fields of northern France and Belgium. By the end of the year, the fateful telegrams and letters began to arrive home. Women and parents back home began to receive form B. 104–82 through the letterbox, informing them that their man was either missing or dead. The new year was to bring a terrible increase in these sad communications.

Of course, the men who had won honours were singled out for press reports, and their stories compose perhaps the most impressive tales from that hell in the trenches. Such a one was Sergeant Thomas Hubbard, who won a Distinguished Conduct Medal in 1915. He was in

The Chums leaving for their training camp. *Lincolnshire Archives*

Chums men from 2 Platoon looking smart in proper uniforms, after a long wait during which they trained in varied apparel and without proper weapons.

the 1st Lincolns, and his special service was in bringing up ammunition supplies at great personal risk. His profile in the paper encapsulates the nature of the typical army man, firmly in that career before the war broke out: 'He was among the first batch of the Lincolns to be sent to the front and fought at Mons, so he has been engaged in the war since its very beginning. He was a private when he went out, but has since been promoted to the rank of sergeant.'

It was not only the Chums who were preparing to fight abroad by the end of 1915. In March that year, the Fifth Lincolnshire Regiment was on active service. They had been organized in 1908 and were given their colours at *Windsor* by Edward VII in 1909. They had been recalled to Grimsby at the outbreak of war from camp in Bridlington, and by late August they had left for training, first to Derbyshire and then to both Luton and Essex. They left for France in early 1916, and were part of the 46th Division.

They were in action at Loos, which the British took and held. It took place from 25 September to 8 October, and the main objective was to take Lens, which was a mining town. Loos, along with an important position known at Hill 70, was to the east.

Of their many casualties, it is hard to find one that is most tragically typical of the sacrifice of the young men of that generation in war than the story of Private John Picksley, who was just twenty-one when he was killed at that Loos engagement, first being reported missing, with all the usual following grief experienced at home. In a feature on John Picksley in the *Grimsby Telegraph* special issue on the war, research by the soldier's niece, Joan Smith, was highlighted. John was in the 1/5th Lincolns, and his experience of war in that battle included the first use of gas, another factor to consider. Joan tells a fuller story about her uncle:

> When John went off to the war he was like all the others. They thought it was going to be wonderful. They came from a village and worked on farms but at that age they had had hardly any life. Then John came back on leave a totally changed person. He would suffer from boils. He was in a right state. His mum tried to build him up but he went back to the front and got blown up.

They saw action again at the notorious Ypres Salient, and then, later, at the Hohenzollern Redoubt on 13 October. The latter engagement brought terrible losses: from 850 in the assault, only 129 men were unharmed. They were later sent to Egypt, and then recalled, and they were in battle at Vimy Ridge.

The men who had already been professional soldiers and who had been sent to France in the first British Expeditionary Force experienced great losses from their ranks as well, and in 1915, reports on their deaths were regular pieces in the local papers. Some were fully reported, and so we learn a lot about their nature and contributions. This is the case with Sapper E.J. Bell, for instance, whose death was reported in April. The feature includes a letter from his CO, in which we have this:

> Dear Mrs Bell,
>
> I am very sorry to tell you that your husband, No. 14784 Sapper E.J. Bell, was killed in action this afternoon. We had to assist the infantry to seize some post that the Germans had captured a few days before. It was while we were working up at the post that he was killed. Your husband has been in my section ever since the war started, and I am very sorry to lose him. He was always very

cheery about his work and I am certain that I will never meet with a better man for doing a job.

About his work today, I may say that he and two other Sappers were building up a place for the infantry to fire from. The Germans opened fire on the post with a machine gun. He was killed, shot through the heart, and the other two were wounded. We managed to get all three away and he is buried in a field behind the firing line.

This is that rare document, a letter written from the front, in the midst of the slaughter, from an officer who cared – about his soldier and about the man's wife. She, unlike so many, knew something about how her man died and what happened to him.

By late October in that year, the Grimsby War Hospital Supply Depot was established. This was one of the real success stories of the war. The publication *Grimsby's War Work*, issued in 1919, pointed out that 'No war work struck the local imagination with such force' as this place and its workers. The booklet added, 'Here ladies were giving up their time, day after day, month after month, year after year, for the sake of the wounded; were plying their needles to make bandages and swabs, and all kinds of dressings and comforts for the broken soldiers and sailors.'

Leading the work at the depot was Lady Bennett, and she and her women met one particular challenge, in March 1918, when dressings were urgently needed after an Allied retreat. *Grimsby's War Work* describes their response: 'Did these ladies, who had been working for two and a half years, murmur? Not a bit of it. Their reply was, "We will work every day and on Sundays."'

During its period of work, the depot, based at Welholme House, made 198,064 articles, including 1,118 pyjama suits, and also ninety pairs of crutches and forty-six shrouds. Someone at the council even worked out the value of goods made, and gave this as being £6,216 3s. 6d. The parcels of hospital equipment were sent out to 115 hospitals, clearing stations and so on, and not only to the Western Front but to Salonica, where the Lincolnshire Yeomanry served in 1915.

Added to this was the Grimsby Women's Emergency Corps, and in 1915 it was in full swing, having sent out presents and clothes to the front. In early 1915, as the *Grimsby Telegraph* reported, there was a hearty response to the women's gifts of Christmas boxes. One typical letter runs: 'Dear Madam, The Officer Commanding the 1st Battalion Coldstream Guards has asked me to write and thank the women of Grimsby for the splendid gift of clothing and comforts … they have arrived safely and have been distributed to the NCOs.'

Chapter Three

1916: Total Commitment

One historian has called 1916 'A new kind of Hell'. It entailed the escalation of the war at sea, the Battle of the Somme and the spread of the conflict in the air, in which men involved did not expect to live more than the next week. Certain particular confrontations were horrendous, such as the fight at Mametz Wood in which there were about 4,000 casualties, or the deaths of 8,000 Australian troops at Pozières Ridge.

On top of all that, there was the desperate need for new men to fight, after the losses of great numbers of professional soldiers in the first phase of the war. Hence, conscription arrived, with all its divisions and emotional turmoil.

Another significant development – one involving Lincolnshire – was the despatch of the first tanks to France, from the Lincoln Foster works. In 1914 there had been oil-engined tractors sent out, and then in 1915 what was called the 'land ship' was created, and a version called Little Willie was subjected to trials at Hatfield. By September 1916 there were supposed to be fifty tanks sent out to the war, although in fact only thirty-two arrived.

In November, *The Daily Mirror* presented its readers with a picture of a tank, and found it a struggle to explain what it was, making it sound more like a monster than anything man-made: 'Today we are able to publish the first photograph of one of his Majesty's land ships. … This "juggernaut", this "Diplodocus", to give it but two of the hundred and one names … was seen "galumphing" into action.'

As 1916 opened, there was a hardening awareness that times were tough and getting tougher, in all senses. The demands for survival and for continuing the aggression against the enemy were evident to everyone, on the home front as in the trenches, on the seas and in the air. The popular magazine *The People's Friend* expressed a common view, exhorting everyone's efforts:

Now that the Government is restricting the use of paper, sugar, fruit and other commodities, and the railways are beginning to cut down their services, it is evident that we are going to feel the pinch of war-time conditions more acutely; but if these restrictions are

Old Humberstonians' Roll of Honour.

[REVISED LIST.]

KILLED IN ACTION (OR
DIED OF WOUNDS).

Officers :

LIEUT. L. P. ABBOTT, Leicester
Regt.
SEC.-LIEUT. C. O. BELL, Beds.
Regt.
SEC.-LIEUT. J. COULSON, Lincs.
Regt.
LIEUT. R. EASON, Lincs. Regt.
LIEUT. L. FALKNER, Lincs. Regt.
FLIGHT-LT. E. G. RIGGALL, R.N.A.S.
SEC.-LIEUT. G. ROBINSON, Middlesex Regt.
SEC.-LIEUT. J. H. WADDINGTON, Welsh Regt.

N.C.O.'s and Privates :

LANCE-CORPL. T. J. CROFT, Middlesex Regt.
PTE. H. FRYMAN, Royal Scots.
PTE. J. W. GODDARD, Lincs. Regt.
LANCE-CORPL. C. GREENAWAY, Lincs. Regt
PTE. P. LEESON, Lincs. Regt.
PTE. B. W. TAYLOR, Lincs. Regt.
PTE. R. THOMPSON, Lincs. Regt.

NOW SERVING.

Officers :

LIEUT. A. BANNISTER, Lincs. Regt.
SEC.-LIEUT. J. BARKER, R.F.C.
SEC.-LIEUT. M. BARRACLOUGH, Lancs. Hussars.
REV. B. D. BEELEY, Chaplain to H.M. Forces.
LIEUT. W. E. BOTT, Royal Fusiliers.

A roll of honour page from *The Humberstonian* school magazine.
Author's collection

necessary in order that we may win the war, no one will complain.

The hard work and shortages were affecting almost everyone, and this was to last through the next few years. At the Holme Hill Catholic Day School, for instance, the log book noted: 'School closed today as teachers were helping to fill up sugar registration cards.'

But there was also a strong tone of encouragement and patriotic fervour expressed in all quarters. In *The Humberstonian*, the Clee Grammar School magazine, the editorial had carried the poem *Pro Rege et Patria:*

Masters and boys are we doing our bit
In keeping the Empire free?
Each, even here, may be showing his grit,
Like the lads we sent from Clee.

The first armies, those of regular soldiers, had done their bit, along with the supporting Territorials. Then, in January 1916 came the call for more men, and the arrival of conscription. The total war was to entail a total war effort, and now Kitchener's Pals Regiments were sorely needed, along with even more men, as conscripts.

In 1914, the media had made it clear that the war was for the professionals; everyday workers, young students, men working to maintain young families never gave a moment's thought to the possibility that they would one day be told to be solders. *Told* is the operative word. Throughout the long history of the British Empire, the fighting against the Indian peoples, the Ashantis and the Zulus, the French fighters for Napoleon, the Russians in the Crimea, had been done by the professional soldier, the Tommy Atkins that Kipling had celebrated as the scrapper, hardened in a hundred battles, wearing his red coat proudly and risking his life while the collier, the farmer and the domestic servant went on maintaining the status quo back home. Then, after the shock of massive failure as the British Expeditionary Force met defeat after defeat in 1915, Lord Kitchener and the other top brass of the army wanted more men – men who were not soldiers – and thousands upon thousands had to meet what many later called 'The Test' of their manhood and patriotism.

As massive numbers of ordinary men went to make an attestation in late 1915, they still thought that the day when they put on a uniform and carried a gun would not come. They were asked to 'attest', and that meant simply stating that they would be willing to fight if needed. But then, there were still plenty of soldiers, surely?

Then, in January 1916, the Military Service Act was passed, making

A cheery picture of wounded fighting men at Weelsby camp, at Weelsby Woods, which was used by a number of different regiments.
Grimsby Central Library

it clear that the government wanted men for the great war machine that was set up and digging in across the Channel, in a war that was going to last for some time, perhaps beyond many another Christmas. There were to be several contentious issues around the idea of conscription. In the Grimsby area, not only would there be the prospect of farm workers being called up, but also the possible conscription of trawler men into the army.

The process began with the appointment of Lord Derby in October 1915 as Director General of Recruiting. After that, the Group Scheme was implemented. This meant that a process of attestation was begun whereby men from the ages of eighteen to forty could attest that they would join up when demanded. They were to wear a distinctive armband, so that they would not receive the white feather – the mark of alleged cowardice.

At that time there was certainly no problem with conscription in the mind of the MP for Grimsby, Mr Thomas Tickler, as he asked the Prime Minister in the House if he would introduce conscription for the purposes of prosecuting the war with all the available forces of the Empire, and thereby saving the lives of thousands of our soldiers by 'bringing the war to a speedy and successful end'.

A typical Grimsby example is the story of John Baxter, who signed a short service attestation form on 2 February 1916. He was willing to be enlisted, and named the London Scottish as his desired regiment, although he was eventually enlisted to the Army Service Corps, which arranged and supervised transport and supplies behind the lines (they were jocularly known as 'Ally Sloper's Cavalry' after the popular cartoon character). Baxter's oath on attestation was 'to be faithful and bear true allegiance to His Majesty King George the Fifth' and that he would 'observe and obey all orders of His Majesty … and of the generals and officers set over me'. His agreement was sought upon conditions of service set out in great detail, including, 'for the duration of the War, at the end of which you will be discharged with all convenient speed. You will be required to serve for one day with the colours and the remainder of the period in the Army reserve.' There was even a sentence asking him to agree, if working in support services, to serve for up to six months after the end of hostilities, and in fact Baxter did just that.

In some places, the dilemma of men who had not enlisted was a fearful one. In Leeds, for instance, as William Herbert Scott recalled, this happened in September 1916:

The main central thoroughfares were crowded. Queues were waiting at the doors of the theatres and music halls. … Suddenly a strong contingent of police, accompanied by a stronger force of military, drew a cordon round, and all men who looked younger than forty years were accosted and asked to produce their registration cards, exemption or rejection certificates.

Common sense dictated that fishermen should be allocated to be part of the Royal Naval Reserve, but what happened was that men went to work on the ships to avoid conscription. This further complicated the subject of conscientious objection and the perceived avoidance of conscription for a wide variety of reasons. Conscription put in place the tribunal. A man wanting exemption from military service had to appeal within ten days of attestation, and the Group Scheme was up and running again in early January 1916. For the usual recruits, the system was that they would have a medical examination in Lincoln and proceed to their postings.

There had been heated discussion the year before, with on one occasion a properly organized debate, advertised in this way:

CONSCRIPTION: DO WE NEED IT?

A DEBATE on the above subject will take place at the Social Union Adult School, Albert Street, On Saturday Jan 16th. At 7.30 pm between Mr Balmforth (affirmative) and Mr Sowden (negative)

Admission free. Refreshments. Open discussion.

The tribunals were bones of contention. They would be panels of dignitaries, with a military man amongst them, and they were appointed by the crown. One source of problems was the bias and exploitation of local vested interests when it came to issuing exemptions. A few local cases made the headlines in this respect. First there was Rex v Grimsby Section of the Lincolnshire Appeal Tribunal in October. This was an appeal of a wheelwright called Stubbins to challenge the refusal of an exemption order made at Grimsby. Stubbins had been on the tribunal panel in Winterton. He was given an exemption certificate when he stepped back from his chairmanship at Winterton. Then the military man on the tribunal challenged that decision; he had to complete some forms, and they were not available on time, so he merely gave a list of names he wanted to appeal against – so that Stubbins would have to be conscripted. But at the London Court of Appeal, the decision went Stubbins's way.

The whole topic of conscientious objection led to some dramatic and sometimes horrendous cases, perhaps most outrageously in the story of James Brightmore, who was from Manchester. He found himself in the Council House at Cleethorpes in July 1917 for refusing to obey an order. He had already suffered such ignominy that his case had reached Parliament and 'some officers involved had retired.' In June of that year he had refused to assemble his equipment and witnesses from the army had testified to that effect. He argued that the order was illegal and indeed 'unusual'.

Earlier that year he had been sentenced to nine months in Lincoln prison (later reduced to six) for an offence 'committed as a conscientious objector'. From that point there had been a campaign against him, lasting from the January up to his appearance in July. First he was asked to pick up waste paper and he refused. He was given twenty-three days' solitary confinement and his officer had said to him, 'I'll make it so damned uncomfortable for you that you will be glad to start soldiering for your own protection.' A reign of terror began.

Brightmore's tormentor, Captain McBean, said, 'Give him Devonport rations and let him cook them himself. Put him among the Expeditionary Force men but don't let him mix with them. He isn't fit to associate with soldiers. Cut his buttons and badges off … he is a disgrace to them.' It is not clear whether the officer meant by 'Devonport rations' that the man should be tied up or whether he simply meant he should be given meagre food, as implied by the old myth about 'Debon's share', meaning the very worst leftovers. But whatever his meaning, a terrible and hateful regime of punishment began against Brightmore.

The victim was taken to a hole that had been dug to a depth of 4 feet and he was left to stand there; later that same day it was deepened to 7 feet. He was left there, and he refused food. The next day the hole was deepened and he had to remain there; he was soon standing in water. Brightmore's account was:

> I spent most of the day in the hole, water accumulating until it was ankle-deep. I refused food that day. Next morning, 30 June, they came and took another 2 feet of mud and clay out of the hole. I found my strength failing and ate some bread and margarine. It rained and I was wet through but at night a corporal let me out and let me sleep in a marquee.

The corporal was severely reprimanded for his act of humanity. The punishment continued, even to the point of the officer providing a piece of wood for the victim to stand on: a pathetic attempt to limit the suffering, but it was no help. Then Brightmore was hauled before a medical officer.

By that time Brightmore was becoming more determined to take on his tormentor and be uncooperative whenever he could, so he refused the medical inspection. The officer did not enforce the examination, so the doctor merely looked at the prisoner and said he looked fit, and he was then passed as fit. Again, after eating some beans and meat, another day passed in the hole. One man let him go to the marquee but again he was sent back to the hole. He was left in the water, at the bottom of the hole, for another four days, in the bitter east wind. He said, 'During Thursday night I dozed a bit, but my limbs ached so that I could not sleep. I was in a state of collapse by morning, and asked to see a doctor.'

It is amazing to read that Brightmore was then taken before a senior officer, still in his soaking clothes. He was asked if he had any cause for complaints and he chose that moment to go through the awful treatment he had received. The only effect this had was that he was taken to the guard tent rather than the hole, still in his wet clothes.

The real bone of contention – that Brightmore insisted that a conscientious objector should not be treated as a soldier – escalated the situation when McBean asked to see him and told him that he would be treated as a soldier. By the time of that interview, the poor man had been in the hole for eleven days. It was not long after that that he refused to assemble his equipment, not defining himself as 'a soldier'. As he stood in the court in July, he said again that he could not be punished for a military offence, since he was not a soldier.

McBean had become seriously ill by that time and he came to the enquiry from his sickbed in Leeds. Brightmore had known about that and had asked for an adjournment so that his torturer could attend. It was clearly a case of a battle of wills with a sense of deep injustice. The military hearing could not decide on a course of action and the case dragged on. It had to end in an impasse, and so it did, being deferred with no decision. In the end, the only course of action was to remove McBean from the situation, and that resolved matters. But the story is one of the worst cases of cruelty against a conscientious objector in those terrible years when to be given 'the white feather' was a disgrace, and when intellectuals and activists were imprisoned for their political views. Brightmore must have been longing to be home in Manchester, where he probably would have preferred a stretch in Strangeways prison to any more time with McBean in Cleethorpes.

In April the Zeppelins were back, and this time they came for Hull and Grimsby. There were to be more than sixty casualties. Since the first Zeppelin attacks further north, Grimsby and the surrounding area had been well aware that they could be next, and in January 1915 there was work done on creating new defences, including a seaplane base at North Killingholme and also two new airfields.

There had been large-scale rumours of a massive Zeppelin attack back in February. Some civilians, as in this diary entry, tried to reflect on the truth of the fear: 'No, I do not believe in Zeppelins or an invasion. … They are very fragile. They have not even ventured into France.' But the reality of a raid changed their tone: 'Eighteen bombs, it is believed, were dropped in York … some dwelling houses were more or less shattered. One house entirely collapsed, leaving a hole in the ground, while another fell like a pack of cards.'

On the last night of March, Zeppelins attacked London, but one captain – of the L22 craft – had some technical problems and decided to turn and cause some trouble on the Humber and the coast. For obvious reasons, he had Grimsby in mind, being the largest target centre of population, but he dropped a bomb on Cleethorpes, hitting the Baptist Chapel on Alexandra Road. He wasn't to know that there was a large contingent of soldiers lodging in the chapel. They were Manchester Regiment men, and of the eighty-four of their number, only four men managed to escape death or injury. Twenty-seven died.

Locals have left some memories of being in Cleethorpes when this danger emerged. Charles Light, for instance, contributed this memory to a collection edited by local historian Brian Leonard:

> Every so often a soldier would come down the lane and tell the householders to open all their windows, as the army would be doing some target practice on the beach. The targets would be placed at the water's edge, then the canon would come charging down and commence firing.

Charles, born in 1900, is recalled by Brian Leonard: 'During the early part of World War I he was a St John's messenger. He cycled furiously to the Grimsby HQ with the news of the bombing at the Baptist Chapel … he could recall sitting in a shelter at Cleethorpes sea front, watching a Zeppelin fly overhead.' In 1918, Charles joined the Sherwood Foresters.

The accounts of the events of that raid point out that, amazingly, there were four men playing cards at the time of the bomb, and they survived. One information sheet on that dreadful attack describes the funerals of those less fortunate:

> On Tuesday, 4 April 1916, twenty-four of the soldiers were buried in Cleethorpes cemetery, the remainder having been taken to their home towns for burial. The burial service at Cleethorpes was conducted with full military honours, with the bands of the Manchester Regiment and of the Lincolnshire Regiment being present. The twenty-four coffins were carried on eight motor lorries, each one being draped with the Union flag and covered

with wreaths and other floral tributes.

More bombs hit Cleethorpes on Captain Dietrich's raid: Sea View Street was hit, and then Cambridge Street. Thomas Fegan, writing on the raids, recalled that 'The raid prompted some of the inhabitants to leave for the countryside for the duration of the war, but two local lads did so against their will.' These were two men who were suspected of having German blood, and who had allegedly helped the Zeppelins to find their targets. It was, of course, nonsense.

Grimsby itself escaped destruction. Attempts had repeatedly failed when it came to aiming at the town and its installations and naval resources. The closest the Germans came to having any impact was the dropping of a number of bombs on Scartho on 23–24 September. No harm was done and the place thankfully escaped calamity. As the war progressed, there were fifty-nine air raid warnings in total, if we include both Grimsby and Immingham, and there was an incendiary bomb that hit Riby Street. At Immingham a railway signalman died of his wounds during one of three attacks.

There was a boost to morale in September, for the country generally: the first Zeppelin was brought down, dropping on the rich earth of England at Cuffley, in Hertfordshire, shot down by a fighter pilot.

But one Zeppelin, brought down in the sea, provided a Grimsby story of real drama and incident. This concerned the trawler *King Stephen*, whose mate gave the press an account of what happened. The man in question was George Genny, and *The Times* printed a summary of his account, with this explanation of the trawlermen's dilemma:

'The German Commander's manner was suave and polite. He said that if the *King Stephen* would put off a boat and take them from the wreck, he would reward them with gold.' Genny continued, 'Our difficulty was this: We had but nine hands and no weapons. The Germans numbered at least twenty-two and it seemed to us that if we sent a small boat the Germans might attack its occupants and hold them hostages. …We could see no way of rescuing them without taking too great a risk.'

The Germans did not like the failure to effect a rescue at all, and there was a sustained series of press reports and features in the German papers, designed to instil fear of the airships across Britain. One account, in the *Lokalanzeiger*, was this piece of propaganda: 'The report of our Admiralty staff leaves no doubt that the attack was completely successful. The report will produce great satisfaction among the whole German people.'

At the shell factory production was in full swing. On 29 June, as Mr Jackson recorded, 'The lady appointed Welfare Superintendent for female labourers is Mrs Cogswell, a local lady. Her wage was at £2 per week.'

The shifts in operation by then were three: 7.00 am–3.00 pm, 3.00 pm–10.00 pm, and 10.00 pm–6.00 am. The working gear of overalls and caps was being supplied but there had been shortages. In a letter to the mother of some prospective women workers, Jackson wrote: 'We shall be very pleased to make arrangements for your two daughters to undertake work at the factory, but this would have to be on machines. At present we have not any vacancies in the office or as assistants to the Welfare Superintendent.' He added that for the first few weeks they would have to supply their own working clothes.

In 1916, non-skilled workers were earning thirty-five shillings a week, and fitters earned 44s. 6d. As for management, they did very well indeed: the manager himself was paid £360, and a wages clerk received £169 per annum.

A very influential man in relation to the factory was Alex Black, who was born in 1872 and made a significant contribution to many aspects of life and work in Grimsby. Black was a local trawling magnate. His bequest to Grimsby is still funding charitable causes today. In 1916 he gave £1,000 to Grimsby Hospital, and endowed a bed there. At the end of the war he was to offer land to the Grimsby Corporation, and promised a million pounds to match the same sum if they could raise it.

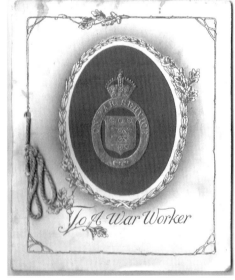

At sea and in the Humber estuary the complications of preparing for war at sea were largely complete, with the new batteries now in action at Sunk Island, Killingholme Haven and Spurn Head. The works had cost £372,000. All along the coast, forces of all kinds were gathered and on alert, and although great decisive actions were often located well out at sea, there was of course a constant danger to craft of all kinds as the U-boats assembled and mines were everywhere.

A greetings card conveying pride in the recipient's contribution to the war effort. *Author's collection*

On 31 May the long-awaited confrontation of the British and German navies finally took place in by far the most large-scale engagement of the war. This was at Jutland, and the battle created one of the most notable links to Grimsby out of the whole course of the war. For decades the German Admiralty had been building up the fleet, cramming their Baltic ports with vessels and developing the naval personnel in very significant numbers.

Admiral Beatty, with a force of battle cruisers, was patrolling the North Sea in search of the German ships commanded by Admiral Hipper. The Germans struck first, destroying two of Beatty's vessels. But Beatty tried to have revenge later, when he succeeded in enticing some German dreadnought ships out in the open to face the British, but the German ships, commanded by Admiral Scheer, managed to return to their base. Casualties were heavy on both sides; one seaman on board HMS *Malaya* concluded his account with the words: 'We lost seventy-five men on our ship and we buried some of them at sea … and my chum went. It brought home to me more when I saw them all laid out on deck. I thought, oh dear, oh dear, I never want that experience again.'

The story from Jutland that places Grimsby as part of an heroic tale relates to Jack Cornwell, who won a Victoria Cross in the battle. This young man of just sixteen was serving on HMS *Chester*. In desperate straits, with everyone else lying dead around him, young Jack remained at his gun position, though he was mortally wounded.

Cornwell was born in 1900 in Leyton, Essex, and joined the navy in July 1915. The *Chester* completed her battle training in May 1916, and as the first events of the Battle of Jutland progressed, the crew of *Chester* found that they were facing four light cruisers from the German fleet. In the engagement, a fifth of the *Chester*'s crew were killed or injured. Jack Cornwell was in the forward gun turret, and he stayed there, expecting more orders. One report claimed that before leaving the gun, he fired one last projectile and sank the German ship *Wiesbaden*.

He was severely wounded in the chest, and was taken with all the other wounded to Grimsby Hospital, where he died on 2 June. On 15 September, he was awarded a posthumous VC. His stay in Grimsby for his last days of life was linked, in January the next year, to Alex Black's praise of Lloyd George, who had become Prime Minister in 1916. *The Times* reported Black's insistence that Lloyd George was the only man in a position of power who was capable of leading the country. Black had suggested that the endowed bed should be the 'Lloyd George bed' and the Prime Minister responded, as the paper reported:

It was announced that the Prime Minister had been consulted and the following reply from his secretary has been received, addressed to Mr Black:

'Mr Lloyd

George is much touched by your references to him and by your generous offer to the Grimsby and District Hospital, and desires me to say that he will be very pleased for the bed to be named after him... The Chairman reported that £1,333 had been subscribed to endow the Jack Cornwell memorial bed in the ward where the boy here died at the hospital.'

On the Western Front, on 1 July, the Battle of the Somme began. This began as a joint offensive by the British and French armies, with General Haig's plans being to go forward on a front facing Gommecourt, a place between Arras and Albert, in the Pas-de-Calais department of France. There was to be a period of five months' hard fighting, by the end of which the dead and wounded totalled more than 420,000 men.

The Fifth Lincolns were fighting at the assault on Gommecourt Wood, after being recalled from Egypt, and after that they were at Lens and Loos. At Gommecourt the casualties were horrendous; the Germans had been at the village since 1914 and had fortified the town and the surrounding woods. When the 46th Division attacked, they faced well-established fortifications. There was a line of redoubts and parallel trench lines. In the action, fourteen men of the Sherwood Foresters won the Military Medal and many more were mentioned in despatches. Among the Fifth Lincolns was Charles Sergeant from Redbourne. He had enlisted in Grimsby in 1915 and took part in the action at the Hohenzollern Redoubt in October of that year, where he suffered a shrapnel wound to the head. He went home and received treatment, but was back for the Battle of the Somme in July 1916.

Charles and his battalion pals had the task of checking the fields for casualties, and were themselves under fire. He was reported missing, and his family at Northorpe Grange did not have his death confirmed until April 1917. He was just nineteen years old.

Other stunning tales emerged later from the Somme battles. One amazing story from Grimsby concerns Charles Carratt, from Holton-le-Clay, of the Lincolns. Having survived the first Somme conflicts, he was sheltering in Albert Cathedral in 1917 when the building was bombed. His grandson, John Major, told the *Grimsby Telegraph* about a silver crucifix that Charles thought 'got him through the war'. John said, 'He believed that carrying this crucifix through the war kept him safe.' As the *Telegraph* report stated, 'Despite spending much of the First World War in the trenches, Charles lived to the grand old age of eighty-eight and died in 1972.'

The Chums had left Southampton on 9 January 1916, and the theatre of war they were destined to experience was by this time a place of extreme danger, chaos and horror. The private infantryman was to carry his full marching order equipment: rifle, ammunition, haversack, boots, steel helmet, rubber ground sheet, bayonet, trenching tool and blanket. By the spring of 1916, gas was being used as well, and so the Chums would be carrying a gas mask.

When many of the first volunteer recruits had started their soldier careers they had been billeted in huts, as was the case at Waltham, where men doing their training lodged in houses, in the Church School and in the Wesleyan school. The Chums had progressed from tents to huts as they moved from Grimsby to Ripon during their training. Now, the Chums were based on the fields of France and in July they were involved in one of the greatest battles in military history: the Battle of the Somme.

Modern readers need to be reminded at this point of the nature of the soldier's experience, with regard to what is now in the history books, in contradistinction to what the actual conflict was like. Peter Fiennes has expressed this very well in his biography of his padre grandfather:

> To them it was a series of assaults, a relentless sleep-starved struggle against the constant bombardment of shells, shrapnel and gas amongst wire and machine guns, bombs and mortars. In that squalor of mud and rain, they met dread and terror, and found themselves capable of unimaginable heroism. It was only those in charge who saw the larger picture.

The master plan of the British was to confront the enemy along a line of about 16 miles, taking some of the pressure of the prolonged fight off the French armies at Verdun. The offensive in its first phase was led by Sir Henry Rawlinson, the man who had conceived the notion of the 'Pals' battalions, with thirteen divisions of the Fourth Army. The Chums were in the reserve line.

One soldier of the artillery, in an anonymous journal, described the moment before the battle began:

> Sat July 1st. Today the big attack on the Germans commenced. Reveille was at 4.00 am. At 8.00 am the battery turned out in full marching order and paraded on the gun park, hooked into the

limbers ready to move off if the infantry advance was sufficiently successful. … Everyone was keenly excited and expectant for now 'open warfare' was anticipated and the beginning of the end.

On 1 July, the Chums formed part of the reserve line, close to the Suffolks and the 16th Royal Scots, who made up the 4th Division. The German front line had La Boisselle as part of it, and here the Chums were to see their first action. We have journals recording the events of this, and one of these was by Lieutenant Colonel Vignoles, who wrote, after being wounded, about the working of the British plan, which was to have a prolonged bombardment of the German positions, and then throw in the infantry: 'the morning was fine and the sun shining, but the enemies' trenches were veiled in light mist … a bombardier of the RG Artillery was working at fever heat.'

But when the infantry attacked, the German stronghold was not breached, not shattered. The infantry were pinned down where they fell after facing the German guns. Another writer explained what happened: 'If you moved an inch it brought a sweeping crackle of fire and we survivors began to realize our only hope was to wait until dark, but that was a long way off. We also realized, lying there in the shell holes, that the Grimsby Chums must be no more.'

The Chums had made their first attack, and as Peter Bryant sums up in his history of their war, 'The fighting strength of the Chums had been 842, so 59 per cent of those who took an active part in the assault were listed as dead, wounded or missing.'

As John Buchan noted in his book on the Somme, written as the official account, describing the Pals battalions: 'In their ranks were every class and condition – miners from the North of England, factory hands from the industrial centres, clerks and shopkeepers, ploughmen and shepherds … college graduates and dock labourers … men whose chief adventure had been a Sunday bike ride.' Many of them, as one anonymous diarist records, were staggering back to their lines: 'There was a strange atmosphere … the guns were firing continuously, wounded were straggling along the roads and ambulances were busy besides GS wagons being filled with the lightly wounded cases.'

The Grimsby News on 28 July reported 'The Glory of the Chums' and presented their response in vague and evasive terms: 'There are many rumours as to the number of casualties that a certain battalion of the Lincolnshires suffered. They were serious but we know that all the numbers that we have heard reported in Grimsby greatly exaggerate the position.'

One of the most poignant accounts of the Chums' experience that July comes from the diary of Ernest Lister, who went 'over the top' on the 1st. His son posted extracts from the diary on the website of the Royal Anglian and Royal Lincolnshire Regimental Association. Ernest wrote this about one of the most trying and agonising experiences:

> Poor fellows lying everywhere, some dead and some dying in agony with limbs and shoulders blown away, faces altered beyond recognition. Others crawling on hands and knees, some making their way along the rear like ourselves. We had to tread over many a dead and dying man but we could do nothing.

In September, the tank, in a new and more effective form, entered the war. They came into use as, in spite of the massive loss of life earlier that year, there was a feeling that their sheer presence had a powerful effect on morale. As Peter Fiennes (author of *To War with God*, about the Great War chaplains) puts it, 'By early October there was a dawning in some quarters that the British Army had the measure of the Germans.'

The Chums were in the thick of it. They were involved in a raid on the Bridoux Salient. The regimental diary has this account:

> A party of the battalion under the command of Capt H.N. Newsum and 2nd Lieut H. Brett successfully raided the enemy's trenches. … It was found that the actual time allowed for the raiding party to complete their work i.e. 5 mins was not enough. … At the time the signal went the left raiding party had actually cut their way through what was left of the enemy's wire and were about to enter the trench.
>
> There were no casualties. It was the last main action of the year, but that did not mean that they were out of danger. They had experienced a long and testing year, in the midst of the hell that was to be forever labelled 'The Somme'. In his diary, Private Baumber wrote: 'A few of the lads were at breaking point.' What he experienced was a friend who was so desperate that he had to create his own 'Blighty' wound: 'Once out of my sight my companion muffled one of his hands in an old tunic … and fired a round into it, taking off two fingers. This was just another side of what I learned to accept, here was a man as brave as the next … reduced to this.'

By the end of the year, it was a time for tributes to be paid to those young men who had given their lives for their country. In December, *The Humberstonian* editorial included this: 'Alas, our own roll of honour has to record no fewer than fourteen Old Boys who, in dying bravely for their king and country, have left us to mourn our loss, while earnestly believing in their gain.' Special mention was made of one old boy, and there were to be several obituaries like this before the struggle was over:

Lieut. L.P. Abbot, Leicestershire Regiment, killed in action on 14 July. During residence he stroked the College boat, played full back for the rugby fifteen and occasionally for the first XI cricket team. He had been at the front a year …was commended by the CO … was loved by all his brother officers, and his men were devoted to him.

At the end of 1916, there were 190 men from the Clee Grammar School for Boys still serving.

There is no doubt that by the end of 1916, the images of trench warfare that we think of today had permeated popular culture and media. Tommies such as the Chums were facing the challenge with resilience and humour, and the result was that through their words we see the tough reality, as in the lines of an anonymous wartime song:

Damp is my dug-out,
Cold are my feet,
Waiting for whizz-bangs
To send me to sleep.

Towards the end of the year, there were important measures taken in Grimsby to make sure that the Belgian refugees around the town were regularly supported. Since the first months of the war, Belgian people had come across the Channel and were in need of help. There were the most narrow-mined complaints in the press, such as a letter from 'An Englishwoman' to *The Daily Mirror* in December 1914, in which she wrote: 'Belgians as servants may sound a very sensible plan and certainly we should be glad to do all we can to help these poor people. Surely, it is clear, however, that if we have one Belgian servant we must have all Belgian. British and foreign do not mix well together.'

Fortunately, Grimsby people did not agree. In June 1916 there was an appeal for a fund organized by Tom Sutcliffe and others:

The Belgian Orphans

We would once again call attention to the direst of all needs: the Belgian displaced people, and their sad lot. This is no worse indeed than that of the people left in their own country under the regime of the German military. There, amid ruin and desolation, without sufficient food and of all creature comforts, these poor ones are suffering terribly. The fund which Mr Tom Sutcliffe is responsible for this district is still appealing for contributions.

There was a meeting in November, and speakers talked about what provisions were being made and how refugees were living with particular families. In fact, as research by Katherine Storr has shown, there had been an official Grimsby Committee for this purpose since mid–1914, and Tom Wintringham had led a debate on the subject at the Town Hall on 6 November. A committee was formed, with Lady Doughty as Treasurer.

By late 1916, matters had become more urgent, and Tom Wintringham argued that there needed to be a more regulated and dependable source of funding for the Belgians. Father Peter Feskens, a naturalized British citizen, had done important work, based at St Peter's. He had come to know Lincolnshire before coming to Grimsby, having been based at Hainton, where he formed links with the Heneage family. Katherine Storr explains what happened in the consequent fundraising activities:

> There had been considerable effort put into fundraising and thirty-two people were listed as donating. Mr T.W.G. Hewitt had given £25 and Lord and Lady Heneage £5 each. Dr Grimoldby had contributed five times. Porri's News Bureau gave £1 and a dance at Immingham arranged by Mr Dennis raised 16s 6d. There were also ninety-two donors of useful articles of which eighty-four were women.

The refugees were dispersed and absorbed, and most people saw the positive advantages of this, as *The Grimsby News* asserted: 'over 150 Belgian refugees in the midst of Grimbarians is an unique opportunity of exercising the primary Christian virtue of hospitality, and now that Grimsby has recognized how great the privilege is of welcoming these strangers in their midst, it is proving not behindhand in sharing responsibility.'

The future was generally rosy for them and Katherine Storr points out that by May 1917, there were still sixty-seven refugees in the town. She also points out that Grimsby provided a starting point for many more on their journey to survival and progress: 'At the same date, 143 refugees had left Grimsby to go elsewhere.'

One important figure in all this effort to help the refugees in their plight was Margaret Wintringham, whose husband, Tom, had led the way back in 1914. He died of a heart attack in the House of Commons in August 1921 and the Louth Liberal Party asked Margaret to stand in his place in the local elections. She won, and retained her seat in the 1923 election. She was Lincolnshire's first female MP and became a close friend of Lady Astor. Margaret not only took part in the workings of the Prince of Wales fund for British workers, but also took some refugees into her home at Tealby. The Wintrighams gave a home to the Michiels family, who comprised a mother and six children, who all went back to Belgium in 1915.

Chapter Four

1917: Seeing it Through

In early 1917, Private Ernest Driver wrote home to his sister in Cleethorpes:

> I write these few lines to let you know that I received the parcel you sent which was very nice. The case had not been broken, it was all in order. I hope Frank [his brother] received his in as good condition but still I do not want you to spend money on parcels because I think all of you need it on account of food prices having gone up. I don't know whether your husband is soldiering or not yet because your letters seem to have gone astray. When I have got them they have been nearly a month old. I want you to be careful to get the correct address from Amy [his wife] she will always let you know the proper address. I hope you like your new house. Do you mind the shop? Does it suit you? I should like to be able to see those fine children of yours. I should like to see Leslie playing with that big girl – it used to be a treat to see them romping about. It would do my eyes good but alas not yet. It will be May before I shall see them.

This tells us so much about the preoccupations of the men at the front, and also a great deal about the conditions at home. It was written at the time when the Chums were about to be part of a grand new initiative as the war escalated and rather changed course, but here is a family man and good brother, showing caring, love and a concern for the necessary economy on the domestic scene, in a time of dire straits.

The letter also tells a part of a remarkable family story. The author was one of eight brothers who went to war. A feature in *The Grimsby News* later has the full account:

> To be one of eight sons who have served their country is certainly a record to be proud of. This happens to be the lot of gunner Fred Driver … and who up to the outbreak of war was an official in the Grimsby Postal Department, residing with his wife and family in 4, Jameson Street, Grimsby. Gunner Driver went out with the first Expeditionary Force, and up to the present we are glad to hear, has served his country well. A member of the Royal Garrison Artillery, he frequently writes to his wife, and fellow members of the Postal

Department and his infectious cheerfulness ... is very much in evidence in his epistles from the front. Gunner Driver says that he has had some hot times, but has always managed to evade the enemy's bullets, whilst in another letter he expresses the hope that Grimsby Town this year will win the English Cup.

Fred was one of eight serving in a variety of regiments, from the Grenadiers to the 5th Northants. Sadly, Ernest was to die in July 1918, and in my chapter for that year I add his full story.

By the summer of that year, Ernest was to be part of a British Army that had manpower of 1,700,000. He was with the British Expeditionary Force, and part of the 9th Corps under Major Bewsher, who was later to write a memoir of his war.

Ernest and thousands like him were soon to see such developments as the more effective use of tanks, the more pernicious use of gas, and a continuation of the reliance on infantry against entrenched positions.

In February 1917, there were several major influential events that would change the course of the Great War completely: the Allied offensive in the north and the capture of Vimy Ridge; the move called Operation Alberich, whereby the Germans withdrew to the reduced trench works of the Hindenburg Line; and the U-boat battles. In that month, the German U-boats were sent into action against any vessel at all, and the result was mayhem, with about 500 ships being sunk by these stealthy assailants. Nearly 2,500 Allied ships were lost through the year.

The result was the convoy system, whereby fleets of merchant vessels moved with naval escorts. Britain had to combat this underwater menace somehow, and technology came to the rescue, with depth charges being used. In addition, there were Q-ships, which were ships of war in the guise of merchant ships.

One way to understand the fundamental situation of a town and its wartime problems is to see what the police have to say, and Grimsby is no exception. In his report for 1917, the chief constable made it clear that the subject of aliens and suspicious persons was a real priority and the work involved had kept his men busy. He had noted that 1,334 'friendly aliens had registered' and his notes show the minute enquiries undertaken. He wrote: 'There are nine male alien enemies in the borough over sixty years of age and twenty-five females, mostly all English-born wives of interned Germans.'

The chief constable's report also gives an insight into the administration that was needed in time of war: '2,193 Change Reports of Aliens landing, and aliens in this district moving to other districts have been sent to the police ... 2,000 visits have been made to lodging houses, hotels etc. To see that lodgers' registration forms and aliens' registers are properly kept.'

Across the country, the process of internment was in full swing, with 60,000 Germans who lived in Britain being gathered into internment camps by the end of the war. In Douglas, on the Isle of Man, there were about 20,000 internees.

The stresses and strains at home were showing through the stiff-upper-lip determination, and the experience of shortages was causing concern. The vicar of St Mary and St James, Grimsby, wrote a letter to his parish in February, in which he gave the parishioners a lecture on manners and required behaviour:

> Of course there are inconveniences, and grave ones. But if only people would register themselves at some shop, I believe they would get their share of what is necessary, and there would not be such a need for queues. Queues are hotbeds of discontent and mischief. I hear ugly stories of the fraud practised by some, who plant different members of their family at intervals along the queue, and large pieces of bread and butter have been thrown away into the churchyard! I would give a lot to find out who these criminal wasters are. Again, when people cannot buy quite what they want, there is far too much wild and reckless talk.

There was also the home front challenge of helping and treating the vast number of wounded servicemen who were invalided out of the war.

An ambulance arriving at Brocklesby Park, which was in use as a war hospital. *Lincolnshire Archives*

Eventually, more than 3,000 stately homes across Britain were to be used as military hospitals. At Brocklesby Park, where the Chums had started their training, medical staff were installed, and photos survive showing the nursing staff in the makeshift 'wards'. It opened as a Voluntary Aid Detachment hospital in March 1915, and by February 1919 it had treated 570 wounded men. Among those admitted were two soldiers from the Cleethorpes Zeppelin raid.

A picture showing a 'ward' at Brocklesby Hall. *Lincolnshire Archives*

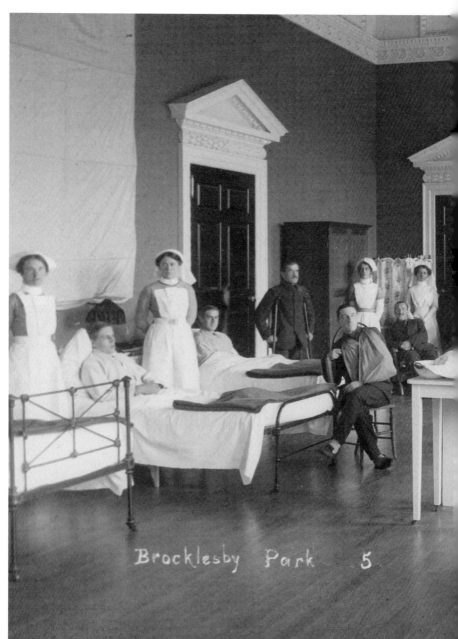

One of the photos from Brocklesby at the time shows Marica Pelham, Countess of Yarborough, who worked as the commandant. The eldest son of the Countess and Lord Yarborough, Charles, Lord Worsley, was killed in action, at just twenty-seven years old, so they had good reason to do more than their share of tending to the masses of young men who had come close to death at the front.

Across North Lincolnshire and Yorkshire there were several similar country houses doing the same work, and men from the Greater Grimsby

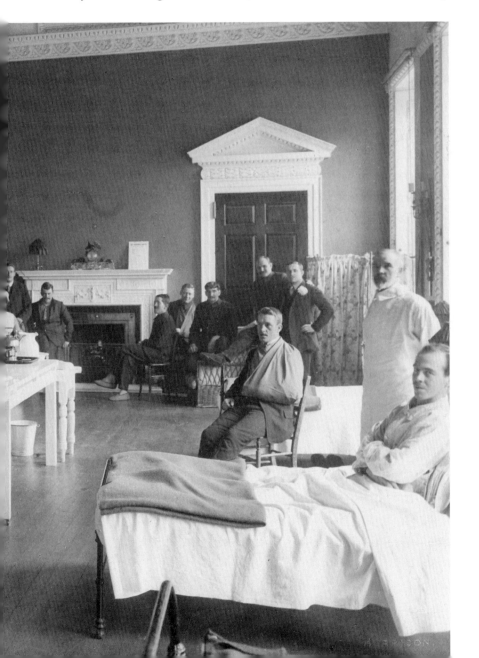

area turned up as far away as Normanby Hall and Frickley Hall. Staff kept autograph and commonplace books, and one such document has maxims and homely philosophy from servicemen, reflecting the mood of the time, such as this from a nurse, in January 1916:

The truest greatness lies in being kind;
The truest wisdom in a happy mind.

Or this, from Private P. Cartwright of the 5th KOYLI:

Here's health to the Kaiser.
The Crown Prince as well.
I wish all Germans were in Germany
And Germany was in ... (well, you know)

But men from the Grimsby area could find themselves in makeshift hospitals almost anywhere, as all servicemen did. One man wrote from Blackrock Castle, Ireland, for instance, referring to the illustration on the postcard he sent home: 'I've sat on this wall all alone many a Sunday night this summer with my thoughts away where you are – ah me!'

A postcard from Blackrock, Ireland, where a soldier was convalescing. On the back he writes: 'I've sat on this wall all alone many a Sunday night this summer with my thoughts away where you are – ah me!'
Author's collection

The war in the air was accelerating in early 1917. In the first years of the war, there had been a very high level of casualties sustained by the Royal Flying Corps (the precursor of the Royal Air Force) and flying had been more hazardous and risky to life than trench warfare, with a pilot having a frighteningly high chance of meeting death at the hands of a German machine gun fired from an enemy cockpit. The records of the war in the air reveal a string of heroes, and many, such as Reginald Warneford, won high honours. He received the Victoria Cross for single-handedly destroying a Zeppelin. There were many more, and some were Grimsby men.

We know a lot about the conditions of flying in the war, as a number of memoirs have come down to modern researchers. One piece of writing expresses the feeling well: 'On days when the clouds form almost a solid flooring, one feels very much at sea. ... Principally our work consists of keeping German airmen away from our lines, and in attacking them when opportunity offers.' Earlier in the war, before the technology of fixing machine guns that would fire through propellers, and before guns were more advanced, airmen would drop bombs by hand and fire guns at each other. It was primitive and extremely risky.

Towards the end of 1916 there had been an appeal for men to train as pilots and observers. There was a strong response to this, and the RFC found itself thoroughly reinforced and well up to strength by spring 1917. Among the flying aces was Bertram Wood, who had been born in Grimsby in October 1898. At first he joined the army, joining the Hampshire Regiment, but then transferred to the RFC in June 1916, becoming a lieutenant at that time.

Wood flew a Nieuport 17. The French pilots had learned their trade in an earlier Nieuport model, the 11 C-i Bébé, and that aircraft was also used by the RFC. Better planes had had to be developed to cope with the German Fokker E III, with its synchronized machine gun that fired through the propeller. In May 1916, the Nieuport 17 came into service, and it was in that craft that Wood was to make his name. One memoir described the feeling of confidence in the later, better planes: 'In their hangars stood our trim little Nieuports. I looked mine over with a new feeling of importance and gave orders to my mechanicians ... to find oneself the sole proprietor of a fighting airplane is quite a treat.'

We have a good idea of the danger involved in flying at the time from the letters of Harold Rosher, who flew the new Bébé, as Wood did. He wrote, just before his death:

The baby Nieuports are priceless. I flew one and went up the coast.

… You have heard me mention Coulson … well he has just had an awfully bad crash at Dunkirk. Riley has also crashed badly twice out there. Ford too, is home on sick leave with his head cut open as a result of a bad crash and his passenger is not expected to live. If one goes flying long enough one is bound to get huffed [killed] in the end.

At the beginning of July 1917, Wood had shot down seven enemy craft; he was promoted to second lieutenant and he won the Military Cross. The citation explains why:

For conspicuous gallantry and devotion to duty on many occasions, when engaged with hostile aircraft, during which he has shown a fine offensive spirit and the utmost fearlessness. He has had no less than twenty-three combats, in the course of which he has destroyed and driven down numerous enemy machines, frequently attacking several single-handed, and on one occasion fighting with his revolver when he had run short of gun ammunition.

When given some time off, back in England in late 1917, posted with 44 Squadron, he had earned the rest. But in one of the cruellest ironies in the story of the Great War pilots, he was to die in a training exercise, well away from the German enemies who were after him, as the British had been keen to pot the great Manfred von Richthofen, the 'Red Baron'. Wood was in a Sopwith Camel over Essex, when the plane crashed. He was killed instantly. One coda to the story has to be told: the fact that in the war he had always had a lucky mascot – a Lincoln imp – with him, and it had been left in his plane at the front.

In the parish magazine of St Mary and St James, Wood was profiled in a group In Memoriam piece:

The death of Walter Bertram Wood, so soon after the death of his elder brother, came as a great shock to us all. … He had only just reached the age of twenty, and had rapidly become an aviator of extraordinary skill, nerve and courage. It was only a month ago that we recorded his extraordinary feats in battle, for which he had received a Military Cross, and recently, a bar. His simple goodness … endeared him to all he met. His was the very best type of high-minded, pure-hearted young manhood. There was a large congregation at his military funeral in church. The choir-school was there, his Scouts and a great concourse of friends.

There were plenty of other flyers from Grimsby who were distinguished by their service in the war, as Peter Chapman reminded readers of a

Grimsby Telegraph special memorial feature. These include Robert Lincoln, whose plane crashed in November 1917, and whose body was brought back to Grimsby for burial. Sadly, his father was to die soon after, and Chapman notes that he died 'after a six-month illness, known to us as a broken heart, and was buried alongside him [his son].'

There was also Walter Beales, who won the Distinguished Conduct Medal. Beales was attacked by three enemy planes while he was on a reconnaissance flight, and even with a wound, he fought them off. This intrepid flyer had an impressive record, having downed five enemy craft. His record led to the award of the DCM in 1918, and he came home to maintain his work with aircraft, being prominent in the Grimsby Air Training Corps.

Peter Chapmen selects RFC flyer Tom Stevens for special mention, and understandably so. Stevens was a man with a musical and theatrical background, being conductor and then in charge of the Prince of Wales Theatre orchestra. He started his war participation by joining the Artists Rifles (famous for being the outfit in which many writers of the period did their soldiering) but like Wood, he answered the call of the RFC.

On the Western Front, the bigger picture for 1917 was that the Germans decided to hold a defensive position. Their creation of the Hindenburg Line in the previous year had given them a less extensive front and made a circumscribed area in which, should the Allies break through, a counter-attack could be made using a dense concentration of men. This also meant that in their overarching tactics, a concentration on the war at sea and the U-boat campaign could be more sustained.

In front of the Hindenburg Line their policy was to lay waste the terrain over a large area, so forcing the enemy to work hard to progress as they were faced with a succession of field obstacles.

The Chums were, by April, at the front line, as the 34 Division was in position, ready for an offensive at Roclincourt. They were under bombardment for days in their trenches, until what has become known as the Battle of Arras began, in which sixteen divisions were involved. The taking of the Vimy Ridge was a major objective. On the south of that ridge was Roclincourt, and on 8 April, the Chums were ready to take that position, although they had to endure more shelling as they waited.

It was clear to everyone that they were in a vulnerable position. Captain Kennington recorded the anxiety, and then the advance: 'We moved forward, keeping a good, steady line, and maintaining direction well. Our barrage was again splendid, although one gun on our right was shooting short and inflicting casualties on our own men.'

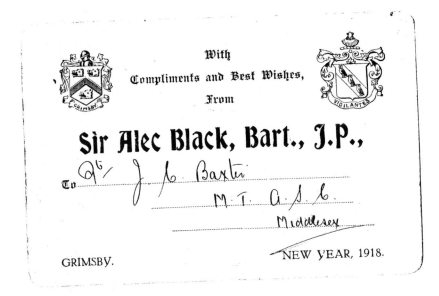

With

Compliments and Best Wishes,

From

Sir Alec Black, Bart., J.P.,

To _____

GRIMSBY.   NEW YEAR, 1918.

A greetings card from Sir Alec Black to Private J.C. Baxter, who was in the Army Service Corps. *Author's collection*

As the advance continued, the men approached what was called the Jewel Line, and whether or not there were Germans in there was a moot point. But luck was with them, as one diary records, and then we have a glimpse of that humour that kept the esprit de corps alive, when he says of an officer, 'He walked up and down, making jokes and imitating Charlie Chaplin, keeping the men laughing. The officer was wounded at this point but continued to display the utmost sangfroid.'

In July, the men would have seen the new tanks in action. In November, the midst of battle at Cambrai, they showed their value: they were capable of crushing barbed wire, and on top of that, with the use of fascines of wood, tanks could be used to tackle trenches and to move over them. The lighter Whippet tank was in use at Amiens in the next year.

By the summer of 1917 there was ample recognition given to acts of heroism as well as to the growing rolls of honour in various publications. In *The Humberstonian*, for instance, there was old boy Corporal A.H. Watson, of the 40th Division Armoured Column, who had won the Military Medal:

At Riaumont on 8 June 1917, when in charge of 2 T. Mortar, firing from the yard of a house. The position was heavily shelled by 15cm and 10.5cm shells, the house being destroyed and the position

An unusual card with a humorous image of trench warfare. *Author's collection*

covered with debris. This NCO cleared his position and brought his mortar into action again and fired all day under heavy fire until 8.30 pm. On the previous day the NCO had his position destroyed by shell fire, but by his courage and skill was able to withdraw his detachment and mortar without casualties, before the position was totally destroyed. At Loos, on 14 May 1917 … in charge of a 2 T.M., was firing from an open trench under heavy fire. His mortar was several times buried … but with great courage and skill he each time cleared the mortar and continued to fire until all ammunition was expended.

The Lincolnshire Yeomanry had gone further afield. In June this year they were at Suez. They were working as part of the Anzac Mounted Division, part of the Egyptian Expeditionary Force. The Yeomanry took part in the first two battles of Gaza, in which three infantry divisions and two mounted divisions tried to take the settlement, which was very strongly defended by an Ottoman army. The Turks were allied to the Germans, hence the war in the Middle East had escalated and there was a constant demand for men, especially from Territorial forces, to go in support of actions there.

8th Battalion The Lincolnshire Regiment.

With Best Wishes.

From . .

Kenneth to Minnie + Charlie,

Christmas, 1917.

The Lincolnshire Regiment.

A greetings card from the Lincolnshires, Christmas 1917. *Author's collection*

The importance of this confrontation in the Middle East is explained by the need to retain the Suez Canal. Back in 1915 a British force met a Turkish army that had ventured into Sinai (Turkey was allied with Germany) and the Turks were beaten at Rumani. Further gains of land were obstructed by the Turks' fortification at Gaza, so in March 1917, General Murray, leading the Egyptian Expeditionary Force, set about the direct attack.

One report of the time makes the conditions (and the reasons for failure in some cases) very clear:

> The outlook was not a very cheerful one, for as far as the eyes could see was dotted with patches of white, which were camps. The strong sun shining on the sand was very painful to the eye and with the heat rising from the sand, made us long for coffee and iced drinks. … Of course I must not describe the defence works but these are of such a character that nobody could ever succeed in obtaining a foothold.

Chapter Five

1918: The Final Blows

Everyone was sick of the war. When would it ever end? Living with it was now a way of life, a habit of thought. Everyone had developed their own ways of coping, but there was more bad news than good, and the bad news was usually about death.

Early in the year, the information about dead and missing kept coming, of course. The papers carried regular bulletins, and sometimes they brought cheering surprises, as in this announcement: 'Previously reported killed, now reported wounded: Dragoon Guards – Wright, W. (Grimsby).' Folk were thankful for small mercies, and rejoiced in that kind of news.

In the spring of the year, the German offensive began, and it has become known as the Kaiser's Battle, or Operation Michael. The Germans, owing to successes on their Eastern Front, transported reinforcements across to form a formidable army for their fresh offensive. There was a massive advance on the British Third and Fifth armies. This almost achieved a wedge between the British and French armies, with a tactic known as 'infiltration' – an intense use of manpower in a circumscribed location. The Germans were, in fact, only around 60 miles from Paris at the time. It was possible to fire the huge guns at the city, and the Germans brought in some of their Krupp guns, which were carried in rail wagons.

It was a truly huge German army that advanced in May: General Max von Boehn was in command, with the Seventh Army, and the First Army had Bruno von Mudra in charge. Their joint force amounted to forty-four divisions, and they were opposed by the French Sixth Army, with three British divisions in support.

The German front line extended from the sea south of Ostend right down to the Aisne, to the east of Rheims. At Lys, in April, the Allied front lines were defended by several Commonwealth forces, including Australian, New Zealand and South African men. This action was defined in part by the terrible use of poison gas by the Germans.

Ludendorff was in command, and facing him for the Allies were Marshall Foch for the French and General Gough commanding the Fifth Army. Ludendorff had promised the Reichstag that the offensive would be a great success, in spite of the certainly of a high number of losses. The aim was to isolate the British, and the chief strategic tool was the German railway system, which, from behind the lines, could rush troops to any desired location very smartly.

The Germans crossed the canal at Oise, and the hard fact for the British was that their fourteen divisions were to encounter forty German divisions; they carried all before them at first, but as one historian puts it, they lost momentum by 27 March: 'The great vigour of the attack had exhausted the attacking armies, their communications now lay across the devastated area and rain was hampering their movements.' On the 28th, they moved forward but were frustrated and it was a desperate impasse.

As that German first assault had broken, the fifth Lincolns were entrenched around Hulloch and Hill 70, facing the German attack, and what followed was the confrontation at the Lys Salient, which the *Grimsby's War Work* publication makes a point of special pride. The Battle of the Lys was from 9 to 12 April, and the German attempt to take a number of commanding positions meant that the assault continued for another month.

Naturally, there are countless stories of heroism and endurance shown by Grimsby men in these battles, and in April 2015, one remarkable story was recently told in the *Grimsby Telegraph*: this concerns Harry Victor Thomas of the North Midland Brigade, who had been in France since 1915, but who was fighting near Armentières on the 18th when he was hit. He told the tale later: 'My right knee was cut in half and a gash just missed my right hip joint and a cut on my left arm caused partial disablement. … I parted with my leg at Amiens dressing station.' He lived to tell the tale, working as a joiner after the war. His son, Alan Thomas, has worked on a full memoir, and he told the *Telegraph* that Harry's toughness and resilience were exhibited in the next world war: 'Despite not serving during the Second World War, Harry still found time to continue his heroic efforts. … An incendiary bomb came through the roof of their home … and Harry took a bucket and shovel and managed to carry it [the bomb] out into the garden.'

Regarding the September and October actions, when the last phase of the war was in progress, the 46th Division distinguished itself (the 5th Lincolns being part of that body) at the St Quentin Canal, action that was part of what is known as the Battle of Épehy. They crossed the canal, facing machine guns, and yet they took more than 4,000 prisoners from a total German force of 5,300. On 2 October there was an assault on Beaurevoir and high ground was taken. Amazingly, 17 kilometres of the Hindenburg Line were breached. 'Grimsby heard with pride the story of the wonderful attack on the St Quentin Canal and on Ascension Valley, in the course of which the 46th Division … especially distinguished itself in the crossing of the canal' – so runs the celebratory paragraph in *Grimsby's War Work*.

There was some unashamed morale boosting too, but it was exactly what the public wanted to hear, as in a piece in *The Grimsby News*, headed, 'Lincolns' Reputation', which told a little heartening tale about the men in the field, quoting a letter from Captain Rich:

> I must tell you one or two things that have happened which show the reputation the regiment has earned out here. One night it was ordered out in a hurry where help was required. A certain general was riding by, and in the dark, said, 'What regiment is this?' Someone answered, 'The Lincolns Sir.' 'Oh we're all right then!' replied the general. … Another instance is what an officer said the other day regarding a rumour there had been concerning the loss of some trenches. It was mentioned that the brigade consisted of certain regiments and the Lincolns. 'Then I don't believe it,' said the officer, 'for no German ever got through the Lincolns.'

On 4 October, the Germans abandoned the Hindenburg Line. Other German retreats were to follow.

At home, rationing was cutting hard and belts were being tightened. Forty million rationing books were printed in June. The year before, rationed foodstuffs included flour, rice, sugar, tea and biscuits. Now, in 1918, essential home baking was affected, with the necessary provisions being hit as well – butter, jam, lard and margarine. We can sense the concern in the accounts of these rationing measures, affecting a society in which such homely maxims as 'make do and mend' and 'make it yourself' were predominant. It is hard to recall in the twenty-first century, when there is such an abundance of both shopping and shopping around, just how much self-sufficiency was applied in the home a hundred years ago.

One Grimsby solder's letter shows how acutely aware the men were of the situation at home:

> That was an interesting part in one of your letters where you mention about having to take your tureen, standing outside the shops, wondering whether you would have to come away without

having secured anything after waiting about two or three hours.
It must make all you women very bad-tempered, especially if it
is raining or cold. I wonder when it will all end, so that the men
can come home again.

In April, however, there was one of the standard British morale
boosters: King George V and Queen Mary visited Immingham and
Grimsby. On the 10th of that month, their majesties arrived at
Immingham at half-past ten in the morning, being met by the Earl of
Yarborough, along with Admiral Stuart Nicholson, with an assembly
of servicemen from both England and France on parade. The French
sailors present were led by Lieutenant Corteville, a man who had
won both the Croix de Guerre and the Legion d'Honneur. There was
also a force of Wrens in attendance.

The occasion was primarily for the celebration of acts of heroism
and great endurance by various people, and the report in *The Times*
summarises this:

the King afterwards held an investiture. More than fifty officers
and men came forward to receive decorations awarded for
gallantry and good service. The briefly worded descriptions of
their exploits … must have covered stirring adventures. Flight
Lieutenant Crouch, for example, received the DSC for an attack
on a Zeppelin; Lieutenant Pollak also got the DSC for an attack
on two enemy submarines while escorting a convoy, and Mr John
Watson, now the mate of a fishing trawler, was decorated for his
successful defence of a fishery section against an enemy
submarine last summer. Many of the crosses and medals went to
officers and men of the minesweepers, of whose monotonous and
dangerous but invaluable work the public hears very little.

The royal pair also visited the naval sick quarters and the naval church.
When told that a large sum of money had been raised for the church,
the king said, 'I suppose it is the same with you as with the nation –
you can always raise money for a good cause.'

They saw the Humber Graving Dock as well, before proceeding to
Grimsby. A notice had been prepared, put in plain view for their
majesties to see, and it read: 'We've done it before. We'll do it again.
A thousand times yes – The Sparks.' They had a look at the gathered
minesweepers and vessels of the auxiliary patrol before leaving.

In Grimsby that afternoon, they were taken by the mayor and
mayoress to the docks to see fish being carried from a trawler onto the

Women doing some heavy lifting, probably about to load a waiting wagon on the Great Central Railway. *Grimsby Central Library*

dock, in baskets. They were met and welcomed by the crowd, who, according to reports from those present, pushed very close and even buffeted the pair. The main duty planned at Grimsby was to meet and honour Henry Newman, whose impressive feat was recalled in *The Times*:

> Newman … was in charge of an armed trawler, when an enemy submarine, after sinking several defenceless boats, attacked him. The trawler engaged until she had only four rounds left for her gun, the skipper's leg was hanging by the skin, and the vessel was holed below water. Even then, he would not surrender.

Skipper Newman was not able to be there: he was in hospital in Hull. But he was awarded the DSC. There is no doubt that the man went down in the local hall of fame, and the story of his heroism will go on being retold, down the years. It exemplified the spirit of the Grimsby men who, while working in their element, on board their ships, were being asked to be in the role of wartime ratings, and in converted ships, of course.

Finally, the royal couple inspected something very much more mundane but still vitally important: the work at the Trawler Owners' Direct Fish Supply Company, where packing and curing fish went on.

There they would have seen the women at work, and had a glimpse of the female contribution to that great war that had exhausted so much of the nation's resources. The workers gave the king and queen a loud cheer, and the royal duties were done for the day.

In that same month, the press were keen to remind the country that there was now a shortage of men. There was a presentation of medals in Grimsby on 19 April, at which Lieutenant General Sir John Maxwell, who was commander-in-chief of the Northern Command, said that the only factor that could prevent an Allied victory was a lack of fighting men. He pointed out that we needed men to fill the gap until the Americans, who had joined the war the year before, trained sufficient men. 'The more men we get, the quicker the war will be over,' he told the Grimsby audience.

Certainly the papers announced the critical nature of the situation, running features on the urgent need for 'the men of 50' to enrol. The Military Service No. 2 Act of 1918 had made men above the age of recruitment now liable for service, and there had not, at that point, been any time period for men to apply to tribunals for exemption, as in early 1917.

There was a plan to summon older men to attend medical examinations; one paragraph, hinting at the desperation behind the measures, was 'Certain voluntarily attested men, who have hitherto been allowed to remain in civil life because they were in fact above the former military age, will be regarded as if they were men whose liability for service had now arisen for the first time.'

In July it was another Tank Week. The *Grimsby Telegraph* announced the arrival of the tank now called *Egbert*, at People's Park. It was a perfect occasion for an array of speakers and a brass band. The *Telegraph* described the occasion:

> *Egbert* arrived sharp up to time at 11 o'clock, and those representatives of the local War Savings Committee who with the official organizer had the pleasure of welcoming him to Grimsby had an agreeable surprise. Up to that hour it was not known definitely by the Grimsby committee whether *Egbert* would be HM T. 141 – the famous *Egbert* – or whether it would be *Egbert* No. 2. The distinguished visitor was found to be the original *Egbert*, the war-worn and shell-battered, looking just as he did when he came back from glorious service at the front.

Egbert had arrived at the Pasture Street yards of the GNR and had progressed through Grime Street, and then had been seen from the best

The visible sign of the aims of 'Tank Week'. *Edna* **was a 'female' tank –
that is, one with lighter calibre guns.** *Grimsby Central Library*

public position, a grandstand view, from Newmarket Street. *Egbert*
had been touring the land, a crucial part of the fundraising scheme,
after starting his journey from Trafalgar Square.

But there was something else looming, something that would
eventually create a huge scale of statistics of death: influenza. The
head of Holme Hill school wrote: 'During Tank Week the school was
called upon to make a special effort. The response was very
disappointing for only 235 certificates were purchased. However, there
seems to be some excuse for this because during last week a great part
of the school was prostrated by influenza.'

Here is the atmosphere of pageantry and parades the Council established to help in the effort to sell war bonds.
Courtesy of Grimsby Central Library, North Lincolnshire Libraries

The Tank Week went ahead, as well as the Sunday School Treat, and Canon Markham wrote, 'Our Sunday school children are asked to take part in the Big Children's Procession on Saturday, July 20th, in connection with the Tank Week. It will be a great function, finishing with a short service in Town Hall Square.' The whole point of the enterprise was, of course, to raise money. Grimsby had proved itself impressive in that activity since the August of 1914, when the cataclysm had started.

There was a prolonged and high-profile press campaign in support of Tank Week. In the *Grimsby Telegraph* there were great, bold-type appeals, spelling out what was wanted, with the exhortation: 'Get ready now to make Grimsby's total something to be proud of ... every inhabitant of Grimsby and district should buy National War Bonds or War Savings Certificate for 15/6 or a National War Bond for £5 or £5,000 or any amount in between.'

For those Grimbarians who were keen enough to read the small print, there were fuller explanations of the scheme, explaining that the money was needed because 'The men who are standing between you and the horde of savage and bestial Huns must be provided with food, clothing and the means of defence (your defence).'

As to how the people's money could be given, there was no detail omitted, and *Egbert* was waiting for them:

You enter the Town Hall ... ascend the stairs ... and buy your bonds and certificates in the Assembly Room. The officials will explain everything you want to know, and make everything easy for you. Then take your receipt to the tank enclosure and have it stamped in the tank itself. [When all this was done, the giver could] be able to tell Tommy and Jack that you have helped to make the Grimsby and Cleethorpes Tank total one to be proud of, and you will have become a shareholder in the British Empire.

The Holme Hill head's log book over the summer and autumn reflects the growing impact of the flu bug. On 12 July he wrote:

Attendance still very bad on account of influenza. On the 15th: Mrs James and Miss Taylor absent on account of illness. Miss Taylor did not resume her duties until 2 September, and she was ill again the following year. On November 15th, the illness was so widespread that the school was closed.

What was this terrible flu? People were familiar with it, because there had been outbreaks in recent times – in 1900, 1908, and even in 1915, when health and strength were particularly in demand. It was a horrible ravager of life and well-being, with its warning signs of sweating, headaches and pains along the back and in the eyes. Even worse, it sent the victim's mood down low, into depression and world-weariness. Now, in 1918, it was percolating through the ranks of the young men returning home from the trenches. Then it incubated in all kinds of places, from picture houses to markets, wherever crowds gathered.

To make matters worse, there was an acute shortage of medical professionals, from nurses up to doctors. The health advisers who were available, at the very top, from whence advice was sought, could offer nothing except the efficacy of alcohol and sleep. The flu took its victims in an agonizing manner, basically filling their lungs and full respiratory system with liquid – some of this being the person's own blood – and effectively drowning them. Desperation set in as well. As social historian Juliet Nicolson pointed out, 'Older people were accustomed to warding off illness and used their own remedies. Opium, rhubarb, treacle, laudanum, vinegar and quinine were all thought to have their own special curative powers.'

It was a reign of terror that summer. Children had a rhyme:

I had a little bird
Its name was Enza.
I opened the window
And in flew Enza.

When it finally receded, the Medical Officer of Health, W. Bulmer Simpson, published a report on the horrors it had inflicted on the town. He explained that there had been two waves of the illness, one in July, for around three weeks, and a second in November. He concluded that there had been another factor:

> One of the most remarkable features of the outbreak was the large number of cases in which the attack was complicated by the occurrence of a virulent and fatal form of pneumonia different altogether in its character from the ordinary type of lobar pneumonia, with which one is familiar in non-epidemic times, and in a very large percentage of the cases the attack proved fatal.

In the earlier regime of the infection, up to 1916, there had been forty-four deaths, and seventeen more in 1917, but now matters were much worse. In November 1918 there were 113 deaths, and measures had to be taken to increase public awareness and efforts at prevention. As Mr Simpson wrote, 'In the early part of December, in consequence of the continued spread of influenza, a handbill was circulated in the town giving directions how to proceed in case of attack and precautions to be taken to avoid attack.'

The press was fully occupied with flu stories, and these were from the tragic to the ridiculous. The saddest were, of course, the deaths of young infants, such as that of Alfred Brookbank:

GRIMSBY CHILD'S DEATH

A little boy named Alfred William Dennis Brookbank, aged 19 months, residing with his widowed mother at 10, Garibaldi Street died on Sunday as a result of the influenza. The mother lives with her sister, and nearly all the family have been down with the complaint. The child became ill on Saturday, but its condition was not serious until early on Sunday morning when a doctor was sent for. The child died, however, before the doctor's arrival.

In contrast, we have the tale of a woman who appeared in court at the same time as little Alfred's death. She was charged with being drunk and disorderly. Her excuse was that she thought she had the flu, so 'she took two glasses of rum which overcame her.' The drink cost her a fine of ten shillings.

The schools were often closed for periods, and as there was an election in December, indoor public meetings were cancelled. It was soon appreciated that theatres and cinemas were risky places to be, and regulations came into force on 22 November that allowed local authorities to exclude children from attendance at cinemas.

The army was inventive, as usual. It created the notion of a 'spray room' and Simpson described this:

In these rooms a jet of steam is used to diffuse a solution of zinc sulphate into the room through which persons specially exposed to infection are allowed to pass, remaining in the room some ten minutes. This process is repeated on each of three consecutive days.

He was not convinced, and commented that the spray room reduced the incidence of attacks.

As usual, Canon Markham had much to say on the war effort across the town, and in early 1918 he was in a mood to quote plenty of cash figures to express a sense of triumph and achievement, but the influenza still hung over the good feelings:

It is a great mercy that the influenza has abated. I trust the doctors will find out some means of preventing a recurrence of such a pestilence. I read that all over the world 6,000,000 people have died of it. But surely the skill of our medical profession will prove equal to the emergency.

But strenuous efforts were still taking place across his parish in January. His great delight was the success of the Sale of Work:

> The mayoress added one more to her many courtesies and kindnesses and opened the proceedings for us. And after two days we reckoned up our takings and found we had made £221, with practically no expenses at all. All the more credit to our dear M.U. [Mothers' Union] ladies who were the backbone of it as usual, and to all the other ladies who helped at the stalls.

Then, on 11 November, came the Armistice. There had been a growing desire for peace for quite some time, and in most European places. The poet Rainer Maria Rilke, for instance, wrote in a letter to his wife about a scene in Munich at a meeting at the Hotel Wagner, at which a young worker had stood up and said, 'Have you or any of you offered an armistice? And yet we are those who should have done so ... if we could take over a radio station and speak of common folk ... peace would come immediately.'

From his study, Canon Markham expressed the jubilation. He wrote:

My Dear Friends,

> St Martin's Day, November 11th., in the year of Our Lord 1918 will always be a day to be remembered by the English race. For on that day at 5.00 am the Germans signed an Armistice, which not only brought hostilities to an end, but was tantamount to an unconditional surrender and acknowledgement of complete and final defeat. By land, by sea and by air. I shall always be glad that I took the precaution on Sunday night of securing that the bell-ringers should be within call.

The editor of *The Humberstonian*, which had provided a commentary on most Grimsby events throughout the war, said all the right things in his editorial in the December edition:

> Peace at last, and with it the most wonderful victory ever recorded in history! A much more facile pen than mine would be required to express all that the two words mean to us during this wonderful week, but I know that the Allied nations have hearts overflowing with gratitude to Almighty God and to all those to whom He has entrusted the task of proving that right is might.

Long after the Armistice, there were still deaths and disasters. Just after Christmas, a few days before the end of the last year of the war, for instance, the trawler *Ostere* was taken into Grimsby carrying the survivors of a Norwegian ship, the *Bonheur*, which had hit a mine. One report noted:

> On Christmas morning one man died from exposure, and another died in the afternoon. The donkeyman, the cook and the cabin boy were nearly frozen to death when the trawler sighted the boat and picked up the ten men. On arrival at Grimsby they were taken to hospital suffering from frostbite and exposure.

Chapter Six

1918–1919: The Problems of Peace

The novelist John Buchan made what is perhaps the most dramatic account of the very end of hostilities in his 1920 book *The History of the South African Forces in France*:

> At two minutes to eleven a machine gun opened up about 200 yards from our troops at Grandrieu and fired off a whole belt without a pause. A German machine-gunner was then seen to stand up beside his weapon, take off his helmet and, turning about, walk slowly to the rear.

But there was a long way to go in 1918 before that momentous event. The problems of peace were fated to be a mixture of anger, uneasy silence and post-trauma stress. But in 1918 there was no real language for such suffering. One respondent in an oral history project once recalled that her mother, who had been widowed in the war, received only the words 'Be strong lass' as comfort. After all, Britain was a society inured to death. Infant mortality was high in the large families and public health was often a hazard in its inadequacies, in spite of the best intentions of the administration.

In short, death was an everyday experience somewhere in a community and talk of it was most likely limited to the same familiar platitudes and the same uneasy silences.

Clearly, there was no sharp renewal of normal conditions. As if to remind people that the war had deep scars, and a tendency to stay around in all kinds of places, just a few months before the Armistice, two bodies were discovered on the trawler *Battle Abbey*, which was sunk in a collision in December 1916. The coroner, Dr Anningson, found himself dealing with a death of two years previously. The remains could not be identified, but the names of the missing men concerned were known. The trawler had been beached about six weeks earlier, but the bodies not found until July.

For a year or more such vestiges of the war would be found or experienced. One of the most challenging and thought-provoking tales of these post-war casualties is a story unearthed in the *Grimsby Telegraph* series of features on the Great War throughout July 2014.

This concerns Submarine L55, and comes from research done by Mr Denis Steer. He told the paper that the question burning in his head was, 'Why was a British submarine sunk in 1919 by the Russians when the war was over?' The men lost on the ship included Leading Seaman Greenfield Westcott, from Montague Street, where Mr Steer's family are from. Seaman Westcott was in the family.

The story Mr Steer found was that L55 had gone to the Baltic to support the anti-Bolshevik forces in 1918 and on patrol, this happened, in Mr Steer's words: 'An officer on board another Royal Navy vessel … described receiving a signal from another ship to the effect that L55 had sunk and that a heavy explosion and firing from destroyers had been seen in the area where the L55 had been seen to dive.' The ship was raised in 1928.

The Armistice and the prospect of the return of peace was certainly no sign of a sudden reversion to normal circumstances. It was as if the nation was punch-drunk after a scrap. But of course, the wounds ran deeper. At the base of everything was the horrendous experience, felt by so very many, of not being able to see, or bury, their dead. Across the Channel, strewn over the fields of France and Flanders, as well as further afield in such places as Mesopotamia and Egypt, were the bodies of loved ones. Mourning had been deferred, and death telegrams had been as terribly familiar as the bad news in the papers.

Those telegrams present us with a profound series of footnotes to a war that seems, on the surface, to have been one in which 'noble sacrifice' was backed by all, except for a minority of pacifists, but the deaths resulted in all kinds of reactions. One woman in an oral history project told the researcher, 'After what happened at the Somme, nobody in our street ever went to church again … where was God?' Another similar reaction is seen in a feature in the *Grimsby Telegraph* for July 2014 on the death of Private John Fawcett of the Lancashire Fusiliers. The Grimsby man was killed at Ypres by a sniper on 13 February 1915. His granddaughter, Lesley Rhodes, told *the Telegraph*: 'My father refused to wear a poppy each Armistice Day … it must have been hard.'

As local historian Gill Thomas has noted, 'More than 6 million men went away to war. This was 28 per cent of the male population. An enormous number of these men were wounded (1,676,037); some of them were disabled for life. Nearly all women knew someone who fought in the war and who was maimed or killed.' Vera Brittain, author of the classic work *Testament of Youth*, wrote, 'On every side there seemed to be despair and no way out. ... Every thought brought nothing but darkness and pain.'

Another memoir, by Methodist minister J. Barlow Brooks, describes the post-war trauma very strongly:

Returned prisoners from Germany – stretcher-cases from hospitals – crippled men and others who had come through without a scratch – we did our best to give them all a warm welcome home. Their stories were varied and their explanations as to how they came through it all were just as varied. There were pagan as well as fatalistic reasons as well as more religious ones. Some said bluntly that their names had not been on any of the bombs or bullets that came their way.

In short, peace had been longed for, and by so many, but when it arrived, it was another variety of shock, for it brought other questions, more demands and most of all, a sudden hiatus in which there had to be an acknowledgement of the need for mourning before the mourning itself was given a space in life.

When the services, ceremonies and memorials did begin to gather pace, they were full and heartfelt, as in this for Walter Goodrich in the parish magazine for St Mary and St James:

It is with the greatest sorrow that we record the death of Walter Goodrich. ... From quite a boy he had helped and taught in the Sunday school and since his confirmation had been a most devout and regular server. ... Faithfulness had been the note of this dear lad's life. He loved his home and he loved his church. And his religion was real to him. He carried it with him into the army. 'We all knew he was a real Christian and he was a good influence out here' wrote a brother officer.

There was also the question of the returning prisoners of war. Since the declaration of war back in August 1914, there had been Grimsby men held in internment camps, principally at Ruhleben, which was about 10 kilometres from Berlin. Possibly few Grimsby people knew much about that camp until the special memorial feature published by the *Grimsby Telegraph* in July 2014 told the story of Herbert Fenwick, who was a stoker, captured while in Germany. His granddaughter told the paper: 'He was on one of five ships leaving Germany when he was detained and sent to Ruhleben camp. ... He was just a civilian really, it was quite unlucky.'

Apparently he tried to escape and was then punished with a spell in solitary confinement. His granddaughter, Yvonne Gilman, has pictures of Herbert, one showing him at the beginning of the war, and one taken in 1918. He looks remarkably well and smartly dressed, not at all like the image we might have of a prisoner in wartime.

Herbert Fenwick's story is one of many from Ruhleben, and we know quite a lot about it today thanks to websites that feature memoirs and accounts of activities and treatment there. Many of the prisoners were trawlermen captured in the first year of the war – men who had been taken while at sea or while in harbour, expecting to go home before trouble started.

The treatment of prisoners was governed by the Geneva Convention, and it appears that the German authorities kept to the rules in most cases. Mail was allowed to be delivered, and cultural and sporting activities encouraged. In effect, what happened was that the camp had generated its own cultural life. One account of the place stresses the purposeful activities:

> The camp detainees arranged their own entertainment. Life at the camp was so monotonous, to relieve the boredom culture flourished everywhere. There were literature classes for Grimsby fishermen, language classes, artists' clubs, domino games with home-made chips and inmates shared their reading material. Plays were produced and concerts arranged. One musician later became conductor of the Toronto Symphony Orchestra.

But Ruhleben certainly wasn't paradise. It was still a prison, in spite of all the seeming enjoyment and community spirit. One on-line commentary points out:

> Personal accounts published later gave widely varying pictures of what then ensued. Some speak of hostility from the Germans, and others of compassion. ... Men from the port of Grimsby figure prominently ... many suffered the squalor and filth of being held in the infamous Hamburg 'hulks' before being sent on to the relative wholesomeness of the internment camps.

One very full account of the Ruhleben experience comes from the skipper of the *St Cuthbert*, John Green. He explained that a U-boat came alongside and guns were pointed at him and his crew. They were forced off their ship, being given five minutes to gather their things. They were taken below and as the night went on, three more trawler crews were taken onto the sub.

Green experienced the hulks. He wrote:

During the whole time not a piece of soap was given to us to wash ourselves, and the ship was practically covered with lice and other vermin. It was not an uncommon sight to see lice on the table and on the rails of the ship … the condition of the ship was heartbreaking, and try as we could we could not keep clear of the vermin.

Green managed to have an interview with the American Consul, and from him he had some cash, so he could buy things to improve the life of himself and his crew a little. They were at first kept at the naval barracks in Cuxhaven, and conditions improved a little. But when Green and others finally left for Ruhleben, he made a point of noting the fate of those who were unable to take the prison life:

One old fellow, I shall never forget … when we left the hulks he was laid on the bunk, too ill to get up and should have been sent to hospital, but he was told to dress and come with us, and the dreary ride, and the only attention he received was from his comrades, was too much for him and he died soon after reaching our destination.

At Ruhleben, it appears that the Grimsby men, along with other seamen from other towns, were responsible for making the camp such a hive of activity. One German officer said, 'You mustn't suppose that the camp was always like this. When the men were first brought here the place wasn't fit to keep pigs in. All that you have admired in the camp they have themselves created.'

With the Grimsby seamen in mind, there was a Nautical Circle, for discussion sessions, along with a dramatic society and a debating society. There was even a football league, with two divisions; a camp magazine carried a page of adverts, one telling inmates that Mr Pearce of Barrack 2, Loft, offered elocution lessons; and one could have a 'first class pedicure' with George Teger, who was a 'professional coiffeur'. It could have been a holiday camp, one might think. But of course, beneath all this recreation and sport, there was the fact that the men were prisoners, and they were cut off from home and family.

The flu hit the camp, as it did everywhere else, in 1918. The field hospital tried to cope, but matters were desperate, of course. Then came the end of the war and it was time to go home. The camp captain, Joseph Powell, sorted out the process of arranging for repatriation. On 22 November, the first party of men moved off, on course for home. The journey, by train, was from Ruegen to Copenhagen, and then there was a transfer to board a Danish ship, at least in one man's memoir, the SS *Frederick VIII*, and from there it was back to the Humber.

The return to normality of the fishing industry presented a very specific problem. There was so much hard labour to be done on the vessels. After all, the many ships that had been adapted for minesweeping work had to be refitted to be once again what they were in 1914 when they were simply trawlers. In addition, there was a general, nationwide difficulty in returning all the men home and back into the trades. Apart from the challenge of unemployment, the men were returning slowly and piecemeal, so there was no unified, steady flow of men back into fishing and shore work.

Robb Robertson describes another problem of the post-war state of things:

> War debris also created problems for fishermen. The sea bed around the British coastline was littered with an enormous number of new wrecks: most were at first uncharted. ... Suggestions that most of these wrecks could be either marked with buoys, blown up or salvaged were dismissed. ... Consequently, a great deal of fishing gear was either lost or damaged.

Naturally, by the end of 1918 and into 1919, there was much talk of memorials. The whole country was certain that something should be done – something grand and magnificent – to mark such a sacrifice. Canon Markham, as usual, had much to say on the Grimsby War Memorial Scheme in his letter in the parish magazine. Being an English project, it had been in the air 'for some time', as he noted, and it involved committees. But Markham was powerfully rhetorical about what the memorial should be:

> It will be a **sacred** memorial. The war has differed from other wars in character. It was a sacred cause. Christianity was at stake. Civilization was threatened. Those who have fallen have fallen in a true sense as martyrs for truth and righteousness. The occasion, therefore, demands a sacred memorial. It will be a united memorial. All who have fought together have formed a brotherhood of suffering and sacrifice. They were of all classes and creeds. But they were brothers in arms and all who died ... should be as united in our loving remembrance as they were **united** on the field of battle. It will be a united memorial for all Grimsby men.

A display of various medals reflecting the services involved in the war.
Grimsby Central Library

As time went on, into 1919, the need for permanent memorials was increasingly felt. Across the land, debates and suggestions proliferated. How should such immeasurable death and loss be marked, and in what form? These were serious questions.

Thanks to work done by Mary Leitch, of Immingham, who wrote *What Happened to Joe? Immingham War Dead Remembered*, we have a full account of how the Immingham war memorial was conceived and finally created. The slow progress of this reflects the national trend, as the projects were done by committee. At first the issues of who was to be included and how the names were to be stated dominated discussion. Mary notes that the Immingham Parish Council made their first decision – to have the names of all who had joined up and then add a clear list of the men who had lost their lives. She said, 'A temporary memorial of wood and asbestos was built in front of the County Hotel. This was not an idea unique to Immingham as the original cenotaph in Whitehall was made of the same materials.'

In 1992 everything was reconsidered and revised: a more permanent memorial was needed. Of three options, the present Cornish granite one was chosen, as opposed to a lychgate or a marble statue. The plan was explained to the locals at a public meeting. Then, three years later, the dedication, quoted by Mary in her booklet, was printed in the *Grimsby Telegraph*:

> The Immingham and District Brass Band headed the procession followed by clergy and ministers, senior day school children, Parish Council, War Memorial Committee, British Legion, Fire Brigade, St John's Ambulance Association, Sons of Temperance, UAO Druids, RAO Buffaloes, ASLE, and F, NUR Transport Workers' Union etc. The Marshall was Sergeant Hallam and the Guard of Honour was provided by the British Legion.

An old employee of the Great Grimsby Coal, Salt and Tanning Co, The Reverend Caleb Nightingale, from Hurst in Buckinghamshire, attended St Andrews Church to speak at that firm's own memorial service. They had lost thirty employees. *The Grimsby News* reported: 'It was not surprising that that the church should be well filled, and among the worshippers were to be seen many of those who for many years have been responsible for the successful growth of the firm.'

Surely some of those present would have recalled that it was the Coal, Salt and Tanning Co that had sponsored the patriotic publication of *The Flag*, as described in my first chapter. The company had played a major role in the propaganda for the war, backing the Christian zeal and righteousness that had fuelled the anti-German beginnings of the conflict. What strikes us now is that there was no irony seen, and certainly no sense of having demanded a sacrifice from their own people. The will to sacrifice lives was assumed to exist from the beginning, in the minds of those who led local industry. It was still maintained as a noble sacrifice, in spite of the many cynical and negative views and opinions expressed about the military machine and its failures after the Battle of the Somme and after so many later disasters. The important thing, as people crowded into St Andrews, was that the deaths should not be forgotten. The urge to create memorials and to speak from the heart about indefinable loss had to be done.

A certificate of appreciation for John Lewis MM. *Grimsby Central Library*

The Chums naturally had to have their memorial service first, well before any talk of stone memorials. It was Canon Markham who gave the address at the Parish Church at the end of June 1918. After a run through their participation in landmark training and battles – from Brocklesby and the first experience of war at Armentières to their last actions – Markham said the important words, as it was exactly two years earlier that they had gone over the top against the lines of machine guns:

> It is two years ago to this night ... they found themselves in position, in their place on the Somme, ready for the morrow's great advance. They were in an honoured position. How nobly they carried out their duty is evidenced by the number of graves in the little cemetery of La Boisselle.

As for Grimsby's own memorial, it was a cenotaph. The monument, made of Carrara marble, was unveiled on 18 December 1921 by Alderman Thornton, the deputy lord mayor. The message is simple: 'In memory of those who died'.

But still in the closing weeks of 1918, there were solemn and rhetorical statements in all quarters as the impact of the November peace settled into people's consciousness. There was a general feeling that the horrors had come close to an end, but while the services were being given and noble words spoken, men still died.

One of the very last Grimsby men to die in the war was surely Alfred Kendall, whose story was researched by his great nephew, Maurice Kendall, and printed in the memorial supplement of the *Grimsby Telegraph* in July 2014. With the help of the Laceby History Group, Maurice discovered that Alfred had died on 20 October, after receiving a wound in his right leg. He had joined the Territorials in 1909, and then worked in Marshall's flour mill in Grimsby. He was awarded the Territorial Force Medal, and is buried at the British Cemetery in Awoingt, France. Maurice told the *Telegraph*: 'The war must have affected so many lives; I can't comprehend how destructive it must have been to so many families.' His uncle had died just twenty days before the war ended.

The facts and figures of losses make it clear that there were many late casualties. About 11,000 troops were killed, wounded or noted as missing on that important Armistice Day, 11 November. It seems to be generally agreed that the last British casualty of the war was Private George Ellison, who died at 9.30 am on 11 November.

At the very end of the year, the editorial of *The Home Messenger* magazine, with Christmas and peace very much in mind, reflected what must have been common to all around the town, with words about heroism but a coda on yet more sorrow. The piece started with:

> humbly we thank our God because fighting has ceased. … The Kaiser and his party are discredited; their infamies have caused a feeling of revulsion to spring up. … Our prisoners are returning home, and we are hopeful that many who have shouldered our burden and risked their lives for us in the field of battle will soon be released from the army.

The writer then adds, 'Amid our rejoicings we recognize the presence of sorrow.' He also commented, 'Pneumonia, followed by influenza, has claimed many victims. We are thankful that the Rev F.E. Ching has recovered, but we deeply regret to learn that the Rev E. Deaton Leonard has succumbed.'

It was a time for gathering the statistics of war as well. The Secretary to the Admiralty provided the figures for Royal Navy losses, and he wrote that the total number of ships of all classes lost from August 1914 to November 1918 was 254, with a tonnage displacement of 651,907. More than 500 civilians had been killed by Zeppelin in the air raids; Royal Navy deaths totalled more than 20,000, and the total war dead amounted to 5,200,000 of the Allied powers, and 3,500,000 of the Central powers. At the first Battle of Ypres, early in the war, in October and November 1914, there had been 8,000 British dead and 40,000 wounded.

Yet, statistics on a grand scale tend to cloud everything. In a work devoted to Grimsby, a more meaningful coda to these facts is to look at the Driver family, mentioned in Chapter 4. In the 1911 Census the Driver family are listed as living in Freeman Street. The head, Benjamin, is forty, and his wife, Ellen, thirty-eight. They have six children, and there are three boys – Kenneth, Lawrence and Frank – who would take part in the war. Other Drivers, from Benjamin's brother's family, would also serve. Most sons survived, but if we have to have one scrap of history from that war that will represent the kind of agony inflicted on families at the time, then suffice it to mention the boys' cousin, Ernest, who had married Amy.

Ernest and Amy had a black-border memorial card made in their memory and the card has two squares of text: 'To our beloved daughter Amy, died 1 July 1918', and opposite, 'Our beloved son-in-law, Ernest, died 2 July 1918'. The flu took Amy and a bullet took her husband. Neither knew of the other's death, of course. There is a Grimsby

In Loving Memory of

OUR DEAR DAUGHTER,

AMY DRIVER,

Who passed away JULY 2ND, 1918,

AGED 36 YEARS.

She has gone ! For ever gone, and left us all to weep,
Till we are called to follow her and in the grave to sleep,
But since she could no longer stay, to cheer us with her love,
We trust to meet with her again in yon bright world above.

In Loving Memory of

OUR DEAR SON-IN-LAW,

ERNEST DRIVER,

Who was Killed in France JULY 3RD, 1918,

AGED 36 YEARS.

To the dead who paid the price,
Made the utmost sacrifice,
Rest and peace in Paradise,
Grant, most loving Saviour.

Two memorial cards for Amy and Ernest Driver, who died with no knowledge of each other's death. *Author's collection*

statistic to put alongside the lines of figures and percentages in the reference books, and not long before he died, Ernest wrote home, 'I hope you are all well. We are not having so many bombs lately.'

Afterword

My subject compels me, as a historian, to try to describe the human situation in the Grimsby area when the surface of life had at least a faint semblance of normality. But even that was an illusion. The suffering would not go away so swiftly. Eric Robinson, a local man whose ancestor fought in the war, gives an instance of the palpable trauma and hardship, even if the more profound hurting was not distinguishable:

> It was sad to see on the street corners small gatherings of old soldiers who had survived the war, and many had suffered gas attacks, having lost arms and legs, or even lost their sight, as did my father. These small groups of heroes with highly polished medals, heads held high, stood in their often tattered clothes or remains of wartime uniforms. Some even had to resort to busking in the streets.

I was born in 1948, and my maternal grandfather fought in Mesopotamia in 1917. I knew him and I spoke to him, but it was a struggle. There was just one faded photograph of his time in that war – there he was in a white shirt and khaki trousers, standing with two mates in uniform. His face betrays nothing. There was an impenetrable silence that filled him like water seeping into a sponge. He was heavy with the memories. His story typifies two important aspects of the aftermath, from 1919 onwards: first, there was the need to feel guilt, and second, that we must add to that the growing awareness that there had been something so deeply hurtful and stunning that no words could assuage things.

Somehow, from the point of looking back to about 1960, when I was old enough to understand at least some of the stories and memories I heard, from men and women who had experienced the war, I could see that the whole business was one of immense importance, but nothing went with the spoken words – no films, books or pictures. My knowledge was limited to the oral history. From the first reading in preparation for this book, I compared the handed-down tales to the book-based material. I soon came to see that I was dealing with something mythic, and that needed to be brought down to actual life experience.

In researching and writing this history, I have been astonished and impressed by the sheer immensity of the tasks facing Grimsby people in 1914, and I am equally amazed to record just how massive and extraordinary was their achievement in giving and supporting others. The world war in the Grimsby experience may have been entirely typical of towns up and down the whole country – and that can never be ascertained – but whatever the truth of that may be, there is no denying the resilience the ordinary individuals exhibited in the face of possible invasion, the deaths of family members, and the daily privations of the home front.

My sources, which were mainly the local newspapers and ephemeral publications, gradually assembled in my story a profile of a community that was constantly asked to do and to do without, and they appear to have managed very capably. In many ways, it was the aftermath, beyond the joy and shock of the Armistice, which is hardest to describe and explain. On the surface, the final chapter is composed of what we have now, in 2015: thousands of family photographs, most of young men in khaki looking at the camera blankly. Nothing in their gaze conveys adventure, excitement, anticipation or military daring. There are no scars on their faces, as in the Prussian fighters, who had gathered honorary scars. Their achievements were to be in a sacrifice of their lives or their health and future to the present crisis.

We also have now a gradually fading oral history, its traces still there, in fragments of tales from older relatives such as myself, who heard stories of the war and retain them, passing on the deeds of heroism.

Yet there is something else – a huge library of printed material, to which this book will aspire, and the last thing anyone would wish would be that education loses contact with the human story, and that the books and magazines, the special issues and memorial pictures, would be kept only in museum storerooms. All that may be said in this respect is that Grimsby, and North Lincolnshire generally, has presented a very positive and inspiring programme of events and experiences that will expand the educative material in printed texts. I hope my book contributes something to the already well-established body of historical material available on Grimsby's remarkable Great War story.

Acknowledgements and Thanks

The research for this book entailed enlisting the help of a number of writers and librarians, archivists and enthusiasts. I would like to thank in particular Bryan Longbone, expert on railway matters; Mike Rogers, archivist, and Rob Waddington and Adrian Wilkinson at Lincolnshire Archives. Dave Raper, of the ASSAFA, was very helpful also. At Grimsby Central Library, Jennie Moonie and Simon Balderson were of great assistance in producing the illustrations as listed below. I must also thank Barbara Schenk, genealogist and novelist, for help with the access to some military records.

Plenty of material came from Grimsby Central Library, of course, and staff there were very helpful in finding sources for me. Particular thanks must go to Dr Katherine Storr, whose writings were a very valuable source on several aspects of the subject, notably on the Belgian refugees.

Special thanks go to the historians of the Chums, Peter Bryant and Peter Chapman, whose books were invaluable in my research.

One source, which stands out to the reader, as it forms a thread running through the chapters, is the reference to the Driver family. This sprang from my own material, acquired in such a way that I feel sometimes that, having come to know the family's war so well, I am almost an honorary member.

Bibliography and Sources

Books
Note: This includes both contemporary works cited and reference texts.

Anon, *The Flag*, The Great Grimsby Coal, Salt and Tanning Co Ltd, Grimsby, 1914.

Bale, Bernard, *Memories of the Lincolnshire Fishing Industry*, Countryside Books, Newbury, 2010.

Barbellion, W.N.P., *The Journal of a Disappointed Man*, Penguin, London, 1948.

Brett, Simon (Ed), *The Faber Book of Diaries*, Faber, London, 1987.

Brooks, J. Barlow, *Lancashire Bred Part II*, self-published, Oxford, 1950.

Bryant, Peter, *Grimsby Chums: The Story of the 101st Lincolns in the Great War,* Humberside Leisure Services, Grimsby, 1990.

Buchan, John, *The Battle of the Somme, First Phase*, Thomas Nelson, London, 1918.

Chapman, Peter, *Grimsby's Own: The Story of the Chums*, Grimsby Evening Telegraph and Hutton Press, Grimsby, 1991.

DeGroot, Gerard, *Back in Blighty: the British at home in World War I*, Vintage, London, 2014.

Dorman, Jeffrey E., *Guardians of the Humber: a history of the Humber defences 1856–1956*, Humberside Leisure Services, Grimsby, 1990.

Dow, George, *Great Central*, Ian Allan, London, 1965.

Drury, Edward, *The Great Grimsby Story*, self-published, 1987.

Ferguson, Norman, *The First World War: A Miscellany*, Summersdale, London, 2014.

Fiennes, Peter, *To War with God*, Mainstream, Edinburgh, 2011.

Gilbert, Martin, *The Routledge Atlas of the First World War*, Routledge, London, 1994.

Gillett, Edward, *A History of Grimsby*, Hull University Press, 1970.

Griffiths, Gareth, *Women's Factory Work in World War I*, Alan Sutton, Stroud, 1991.

Healey, Denis, *My Secret Planet*, Penguin, London, 1992.

Holmes, Richard, T*he Oxford Companion to Military History*, Oxford University Press, 2001.

Howse, Christopher (Ed), *How We Saw It: 150 Years of the Daily Telegraph*, Ebury, London, 2005.

Hurt, Fred, *Lincolnshire in the Wars*, Harrison, Lincoln, 1994.

Jackson, Robert, *Air War Flanders – 1918*, Airlife, Shrewsbury, 1998.

Kaye, David, *The Book of Grimsby*, Barracuda Books, Grimsby, 1981.

Kerr, Gordon, *A Short History of the First World War*, Pocket Essentials, London, 2014.

Leitch, Mary, *What Happened to Joe? Immingham War Dead Remembered*, Immingham WEA, 1995.

Leonard, Brian, *Cleethorpes and District Remembered*, Tempus, Stroud, 2003.

Lincoln, Bob, *Reminiscences of Sport in Grimsby*, Grimsby News, 1912.

McConnell, James, *Recollections of the Great War in the Air* , Pen & Sword, Barnsley, 2013.

Pinkham, Lydia, *Private Text-Book upon Ailments Peculiar to Women*, Lydia Pinkham Medicine Co, London, no date given but c. 1900.

Poulton, Fiona (Compiler and editor), *Men of Grimsby: Record of their War Services 1914–18*, (transcribed by members of the Great Grimsby Family History Group).

Pratt, Edwin A., *Railways and the Great War*, London: Selwyn and Blount, London, 1921.

Robinson, Eric, *Grimsby Remembered*, Tempus, Stroud, 2002.

Robinson, Robb, *Trawling: the rise and fall of the British trawl fishery*, University of Exeter Press, 1996.

Rolph, C.H. *London Particulars*, Oxford: Oxford University Press, 1980.

Rosher, Harold, *In the Royal Naval Air Service: the war letters of the late Harold Rosher to his family*, Chatto & Windus, London, 1916.

Stibbe, Matthew, *British Civilian Internees in Germany: The Ruhleben Camp 1914–18*, Manchester University Press, 2008.

Stobart, Mrs St Clair, *War and Women*, G. Bell, London, 1913.

Storr, Katherine, *Belgian Refugees in Lincolnshire and Hull 1914–1919*, Your P.O.D., Coventry, 2010.

Thomas, Gill, *Life on all Fronts*, Cambridge University Press, 1989.

Triggs, Les, with Hepton, David & Woodhead, Sid, *Grimsby Town: A Complete Record*, Breedon, Derby, 1989.

Triplow, Nick, *et alia, The Women They Left Behind*, Fathom Press, Grimsby, 2009.

Tyson, Doreen, *Grimsby Fishermen who were Lost or Died at Sea*, North East Lincolnshire Libraries, Grimsby, 2008.

Zweig, Stefan, *The Society of the Crossed Keys* (autobiography included, published in 1940), Pushkin Press, London, 2014.

Periodicals and Ephemera/ Special Publications

Aeroplane Spotter, The, Vol. VII, No. 168, 10 August 1946.

Batchelor, Simon, 'Railway Marine Staff among First Prisoners of War', blog for the National Railway Museum, 12 March 2014.

Bygones, Grimsby Telegraph supplement No. 261, 9 December 2014.

Chapman, Peter, 'They Were the Magnificent Men in Flying Machines', *Grimsby Telegraph* special supplement, July 2014.

Fay, Sir Sam, *Immingham: what the port offers*, no publisher, date c. 1920.

'First World War', *Grimsby Telegraph* special supplement, July 2014.

Green, John, 'Personal Account of John Green, Skipper of S.T. *St Cuthbert*' at www.centenarynews.com

Grimsby Official Guide, 1920.

Grimsby's War Work, compiled by the town clerk in 1919, Grimsby Corporation; nb this was reprinted by the Lincolnshire GenWeb in 2009, available online at www.rootsweb.ancestry.com/englin/mem/grimsby.htm

Grimsby Telegraph, special supplement on First World War, 31 July 2014.

Humberstonian, The, Clee Grammar School magazine, No. 4, December 1918.

Immingham: 100 Years of Port and Town, Grimsby Telegraph supplement, 9 July 2012.

Mathison, Phil, 'Hull, Holderness and the Hobbits', *The Dalesman*, pp.45–47, January 2015.

Rilke, Rainer Maria, 'Letter to his wife, 1918', reprinted in *The Guardian*, 12 July 2014.

Simpson, W. Bulmer, *The Annual Report on the Health of the County Borough and Port of Grimsby*, Roberts and Jackson, Grimsby, 1915.

St James' Magazine, October 1914.

Storey, Neil, 'Shell-Shocked', *Family Tree Magazine*, pp. 16–19, May 2008.

Storr, Dr Katherine, 'Enlistment, Conscription, Exemptions, Tribunals' at www.southhollandlife.com.

Storr, Dr Katherine, Producing Munitions, at www.southhollandlife.com.

'The Point of No Return', *Telegraph Magazine*, 2 August 2014.
The Royal Anglian and Royal Lincolnshire Regimental Association: '930 Private Alfred Lister: 10th Lincolnshire Regiment (Grimsby Chums)' at www.thelincolnshireregiment.org/ernest_lister.shtml
World War I Day by Day, Content Partners Ltd, London, 2014.
York Museums Trust project *1914 in Yorkshire*, York Museums Trust, 1914.

The Times Digital Archive

'Captive in a German Liner: A Grimsby Skipper's Diary' 8 Sept. 1914: 3   Web 10 December. 2014
'Dogger Bank Raids', p.5, issue 40847, 6 May 1915.
'England in Time of War XVII – Great Grimsby: Captains Courageous', 12 January 1915, Web 12 December 2014.
'King at Grimsby', issue 41761, 11 April 1918.
'More Grimsby Losses', 11 June 1915, Web 12 December 2014.
'Motor Ship Sunk by Mine', issue 41983, 28 December 1918.
'The Men of 50', issue 41769, 20 April 1918.
'The Wrecked Airship', issue 41082, 5 February 1916.

Maps and Plans

Grimsby 1903–1908, Cassini Maps, 2007.

Websites

Blog.nrm.org.uk/
www.library:nelincs.gov.uk/web/arena/ruhleben
www.thelincolnshireregiment.org

Index

Abbot, Lt L.P., 75
Addison, Christopher, 46
Admiral of Patrols, 30
Admiralty, 40
Aliens Restriction Act, 26
Amphion, HMS, 8
Argo Steamship Co, 42
Army Service Corps, 63
Artillery Barracks, 21

Barbellion, W.N.P., 6
Batchelor, Simon, 28
Battle Abbey (trawler), 103
Baxter, John, 63
Beales, Walter, 75
Beatty, Adm, 70
Belgian orphans, 75–6
Belgian refugees, 74–6
Belgium, 15
Bell, E.J., 58–9
Bell, Lt Col., 34
Bennett, Maj, 17
Beresford, Lord Charles, 27
Black, Alex, 69
Blackrock Castle, 82
Blunt, W.S., 3, 5
Bremen, 3
Brewster's Millions, 47
Brightmore, James, 64–5
British Expeditionary Force, 31, 57
Brittain, Vera, 104
Brocklesby Park, 23, 53, 79, 80–1
Brooks, J. Barlow, 105
Buchan, John, 73, 103
Buckingham Palace, 7, 8

Cambrai (battle), 86

Campbell, Scott, 47
Cardwell reforms, 11
Carratt, Charles, 71–2
Chapman, Peter, 43, 85
Chums, Grimsby new regiment, 8,
    18–19, 20–1, 22, 23, 54–5,
    56–7, 72–3
Cleethorpes, 50, 64, 65, 67
Coal, Salt and Tanning Co, 110
Conscription, 54–5
Cornwell, Jack, 70–1
Crosby, Col Harry, 13

Daily Mirror, 59
Defence of the Realm Act
    (DORA), 39
Dietrich, Capt, 68
Doig, J.S., 33
Doughty Road, 13
Dow, George, 28
Dowsing buoy, 28
Dreadnoughts, 8
Driver, Ernest, 77
Driver family, 113

Eastern Front, 14, 89
Edna (tank), 95
Edward VII, 56
Egbert (tank), 94–5
Egypt, 71
Egyptian Expeditionary
    Force, 87
Ellison, George, 112
Emergency Committee, 38
Empire Fair, 10
Épehy, Battle of, 90
Erander (spy), 41

Falkner, L., 34
Fay, Sam, 9
Fenwick, Herbert, 105–106
Feskens, Father Peter, 73
Fiennes, Peter, 73
Filbert, Pte, 9
Fleming, F.H., 53
Formo (trawler), 35

Geneva Convention, 106
Genny, George, 68
George, Lloyd, 45, 70
George V, 7, 92, 94
Goodrich, Walter, 105
Great Central Railway (GCR), 9
    steamers, 7
    vessels, 28
Green, John, 106
Greetings cards, 69, 86, 88
Grimsby Novelty House, 7
Grimsby Royal Dock, 24–5
Grimsby Telegraph, 8
Grimsby Town FC, 47
Grimsby War Hospital, 58, 69, 70
Grimsby War Memorial Scheme,
    108
Grimsby Women's Emergency
    Corps, 58
Grimsby's War Work, 11
Group Scheme (conscription), 64

Hague Convention, 28
Healey, Denis, 8
Heneage, Capt, 26
Hindenburg Line, 79
Hitzen, William, 43
Holme Hill School, 95
Home Messenger, 112
Hubbard, Sgt Thomas, 53
Humber Graving Dock, 92

Humberstonian, The, 60, 61, 74,
    101

Immingham, 92
Imperialist (trawler), 28
Influenza, 98–100
Isle of Man, 79

Jackson, Mr, 69
Jutland, Battle of, 70

Kaiser Wilhelm Der Grosse
    (German warship), 32
Kell, Vernon, 41–2
Kendall, Alfred, 112
Kendall, Maurice, 112
Killingholme Haven, 69
Kilmarnock, HMS, 29
King Stephen (trawler), 68
Kitchener, Lord, 11, 12, 19–20, 50,
    61
Knott and Baker, 52

La Boiselle, 73
Laming, George, 39
Lancashire Fusiliers (3rd), 14
Leitch, Mary, 109–10
Leonard, Brian, 67
Liège, 22
Light, Charles, 67
Lincoln Artillery Volunteers, 9, 12
Lincoln Assizes, 40
Lincolnshire Yeomanry, 58, 87
Lister, Frank, 50
Little Willie (tank), 59
Lock Hill, 21
Lokalanzeiger, 68
Lord Derby, 63
Lord Howick (trawler), 37
Louth Liberal Party, 76

Ludendorf, Gen, 89
Lullington (steamer), 36
Lusitania, RMS, 43

McBean, Capt, 65
Mametz Wood, 59
Markham, Rev Canon, 18, 100,
    101, 108, 112
Maxwell, Sir John, 94
Mayor's Relief Fund, 15
Medals, 92, 94, 109, 115
    Distinguished Conduct Medal,
        53, 85
    Military Medal, 71, 86
    Territorial Force Medal, 112
Memorials, 85, 105, 108, 109–10,
    113–14, 116
    (*see also*, Cornwell Jack)
Military Service Act (1916), 61
Military Service Act (1918), 94
Miller, Isaac, 37
Ministry of Agriculture and
    Fisheries, 27
Ministry of Munitions, 50
Mitchell, H.L., 17
Munitions, 45–6, 51, 52
Munitions and Light Castings Co,
    52
Munitions Work Bureau, 50
Murray, Gen, 88

National Auxiliary Police, 27
National Relief Fund, 32
National War Bonds, 96, 98
Newman, Henry, 93
Newnham, Miss, 36
Nicholas, Adm Stewart, 92
Normanby Hall, 82
Nugent, Gen, 26

Official Secrets Act (1911), 40

Olsson, Ernst, 40
Operation Michael, 89
Q-ships, 78
Ostere (trawler), 101
Oxford (trawler), 36

Palace Theatre, 47
People's Friend, The, 59
Perham Down, 53
Picksley, John, 57
Pinkham, Lydia, 34
Postcard, 82
Prince of Wales Theatre, 47

Queen Mary, 92, 94

Railway Executive Committee, 28
Rationing, 91–2
Rich, Capt, 91
Robertson, Rob, 27, 108
Robertson, Sir William, 50
Robinson, Eric, 115
Royal Flying Corps, 83
Royal National Mission to Deep
    Sea Fishermen, 36
Royal Naval Air Service, 26
Ruhleben (prisoner of war camp),
    105–107

Salisbury Plain, 53
Schlieffen Plan, 14–15
Scott, William, 63
Sergeant, Charles, 71
Shell factory, 48–9, 51–3
Shipwrecked Fishermen and
    Mariners' Society, 37
Simpson, W. Bulmer, 99
Smith, Jean, 57
Smith, Capt William, 33
Somme, Battle of the, 74–5

Spurn Head, 40
'Spy mania', 40–1
St James Magazine, 33
St Quentin Canal, 90, 91
Staples, Herbert, 37
Steer, Denis, 104
Stevens, Tom, 85
Stirling, John (Chief Constable), 17, 19
Storr, Katherine, 76
Stream, Capt A.J., 33
Suez, 86
Sutcliffe, Tom, 15

Tank Week, 94–5, 98
Tate, Alderman, 15
Territorial Force Medal, 112
Territorials, 7
The Flag, 15
Thomas, Alan, 90
Thomas, Harry, 90
Tickler, Thomas, 53
Tolkien, J.R.R., 14
Torpedo, 39
Trawler Owners' Direct Fish Supply Company, 93

U-boats, 78
Union Jack Day, 15–17

Vanilla (trawler), 15
Vevey, Zena, 47
Victoria Street, 53
Vimy Ridge, 57, 85
Volunteer Training Corps, 11, 53

War Emergency Programme, 40
War Office, 26
War Savings Certificates (*see* National War Bonds)
Ward, Lipson, 41
Warneford, Reginald, 55

Warner, Capt, 18
Watson, Capt A.H., 86
Weelsby camp, 62
Welholme House, 58
Western Front, 15, 53, 56, 57, 58, 71, 85
    (*see also,* Hindenberg Line; Somme, Battle of)
Windsor (trawler), 75
Wintringham, Margaret, 76
Wintringham, Tom, 76
Wintringham Road, 10
Women's League, 10
Women's war work, 43–7, 50–1, 93
Wood, Bertram, 83–4
Worsley, Lord, 81
Wright, W., 89

YMCA, 15
Ypres, Battle of, 30

Zeppelins, 21–2, 38, 66–7
Zweig, Stefan, 6, 21